THE LITTLE BEE CHARMER OF HENRIETTA STREET

'I loved this book! Eliza's courage and kindness shine out on every page in this brilliantly researched and exciting novel by one of Ireland's finest writers.'
Marita Conlon-McKenna, author of *Under the Hawthorn Tree*, *Wildflower Girl*, *Fields of Home*, *A Girl Called Blue* and *Safe Harbour*

'I enjoyed every single page. It's sad, uplifting, warm and sweet. Eliza is a great heroine, and her world of Henrietta Street and the circus will linger with me for a long time.'
Judi Curtin, author of the *Alice & Megan*, *Eva*, *Time After Time* and *Lissadell* series

SARAH WEBB is an award-winning children's writer. Her books include *Blazing a Trail: Irish Women Who Changed the World*, illustrated by Lauren O'Neill and *A Sailor Went to Sea, Sea, Sea: Favourite Rhymes from an Irish Childhood*, illustrated by Steve McCarthy, both winners of Irish Book Awards.

Sarah runs creative writing clubs for children and teens, reviews children's books for the *Irish Independent* and programmes children's events for book festivals and MoLI (Museum of Literature Ireland).

Sarah is passionate about bringing children and books together and was awarded the Children's Books Ireland Award for Outstanding Contribution to Children's Books in Ireland in 2015.

www.sarahwebb.ie

Twitter: @sarahwebbishere

Instagram: @sarahwebbwriter

SARAH WEBB

THE LITTLE BEE CHARMER OF HENRIETTA STREET

illustrated by Rachel Corcoran

THE O'BRIEN PRESS
DUBLIN

First published 2021 by
The O'Brien Press Ltd,
12 Terenure Road East, Rathgar,
Dublin 6, D06 HD27 Ireland.
Tel: +353 1 4923333; Fax: +353 1 4922777
E-mail: books@obrien.ie
Website: www.obrien.ie
The O'Brien Press is a member of Publishing Ireland

ISBN: 978-1-78849-247-8
Text © copyright Sarah Webb 2021
The moral rights of the author have been asserted
Copyright for typesetting, layout, editing, design
© The O'Brien Press Ltd
Layout and design by Emma Byrne
Cover and internal illustrations by Rachel Corcoran

1 3 5 7 8 6 4 2
22 24 23 21

Photo credits:
Tenements at Chancery Lane (Bride Street); Boy with an injured foot; Tenement room at
no 38 Francis Street; 46 Beresford Street, showing some of the remains of the collapsed
houses on Church Street. All courtesy of the Royal Society of Antiquaries of Ireland.
Used with permission.
Text credits
Epigraph from *The Minpins* by Roald Dahl (Jonathan Cape Ltd and Penguin Books Ltd),
copyright © Roald Dahl Story Company, 1991. Used with permission.
Printed and bound by Norhaven Paperback A/S, Denmark.
The paper in this book is produced using pulp from managed forests.

Sarah Webb wishes to thank the Arts Council for the bursary that allowed her to research
and write this book.
Published in

DEDICATION

Eliza's wonderful mum is inspired by and named after my own mum, Melissa who, like Melissa Kane, was also a French teacher and is a keen gardener and bee lover. This one's for you, Mum.

'And above all, watch with glittering eyes the whole world around you because the greatest secrets are always hidden in the most unlikely places. Those who don't believe in magic will never find it.'

Roald Dahl, *The Minpins*

No 16

DORSET STREET

BOLTON STREET

Prologue

Thursday, 1 June 1911

TELL THE BEES

'Someone is coming, Madam Ada, tell the bees.'

Where did that voice come from? Madam Ada stops pinning up her hair and looks around the circus caravan. She spots a small worker bee buzzing towards her.

The bee lands gently on Madam Ada's hand and she can feel the powerful thrum of its wings through her skin.

Then she hears the bee say: 'Someone is coming, Madam Ada. Someone special. Tell Her Majesty Queen Regina. Tell all the bees.'

Prologue

Thursday 7 June 1911

TELL THE BEES

CHAPTER 1

Honeybees have existed for millions of years.
They have been found in drops of amber from the dinosaur age.

FRIDAY, 19 MAY 1911

'Moving?' Jonty stares at Papa. 'What do you mean we're moving? This is our home.'

'I'm sorry, Jonty,' Papa says. 'I wish it hadn't come to this, but we have to sell this house to pay off all our debts.' Papa is slumped in his maroon velvet armchair by the window. He has aged years since Mama died, today he looks like an old man, his face pale and whiskery.

'I've found us rooms on Henrietta Street,' he continues. 'We'll be sharing a large townhouse with some other families. It will be perfect for the three of us. There's a small workshop in the back yard, and there are boys your age in the house to play with, Jonty. I asked especially.'

My brother perks up a bit at this. He's small for his age

and the boys on our road call him 'Baba Jonty'. The more he protests, the more they tease him.

'A yard?' he says. 'Is there a garden? And a tree with a swing? Can Oboe come too?' Oboe is our dog, a black Labrador.

Papa rubs his hands over his face. 'Jonty, please don't make this any harder than it already is. There are plenty of parks nearby. And Oboe's going to be a hunting dog on an estate in Wicklow. It's all arranged. You know how much he likes chasing birds. He'll fit right in.'

Jonty's face drops. He loves Oboe. None of this is Papa's fault; I know he's trying to make the best of things, but the changes will be hard.

Jonty opens his mouth to protest, but I say quickly, 'Jonty, don't be upset. It'll be fun. A new adventure.'

'Why are you being so calm?' he says. He stares at me with his soft grey eyes – sealskin Mama used to call the colour – and I look away.

'You knew, didn't you?' he says. 'About moving. I can't believe you kept it a secret. Traitor!'

My cheeks flame. He's right.

Jonty turns to Papa. 'Why did you tell Eliza and not me? It's not fair! I'm not moving. You can't make me.'

Papa goes quiet, stares down at his hands and twists his gold signet ring around and around on his finger. I know this can't be easy on him either, especially without Mama. People said he wouldn't be able to raise two children on his own, that we should be sent to distant relatives in West Cork, but he was determined to keep our small family together. So I know I have to help do that too, no matter what.

'Jonty,' I say. 'Go upstairs and start packing your things. I'll help if you like.'

He glares at me. 'Don't tell me what to do, you're not Mama.' He storms out of the room, slamming the door behind him.

I wince. His sharp words are like a punch to my stomach. I miss her too, so much. Before she passed, Mama asked me to look after Papa and Jonty and I'm doing my best, but it's not easy.

When Papa first told me about the move last Friday, I begged him to tell Jonty too, but he said he didn't have the energy for a week's worth of Jonty's theatrics.

Like Jonty, I was shocked when I heard. I pleaded with Papa to change his mind, but he explained that we have no money. He'd borrowed heavily to buy printing machinery for his business. When his eyesight started to fade he'd found it more and more difficult to work and eventually had to stop altogether. The house now belongs to the bank and we are homeless.

I went quiet when he told me and I felt all shivery inside. This was terrible news – losing the business *and* the house. I didn't know what to say. Sensing I was upset he added, 'We're not destitute, Eliza, please try not to worry. We have some money to tide us over, but we're going to have to tighten our purse strings. Live a simpler life. I can't do this without you, poppet. I need your help.'

'Of course, Papa,' I said, my voice a whisper.

'I'm so sorry, Eliza.' There were tears in his cloudy eyes so I hugged him, blinking back my own tears.

'I'm sorry you had to bear the brunt of Jonty's anger, Eliza,' Papa says now, bringing me back to the present.

'That's all right, Papa.'

Whack! I see Jonty through the window, hitting the oak tree in the garden with one of the bendy bamboo sticks that support Mama's runner beans. Mama's precious garden – her vegetable patch, her raspberry bushes, her plum trees, the wall of climbing pink roses she was so proud of, and what she called her honeybee bed, planted with lots of flowers bees love – they will all have to stay behind too.

My heart squeezes thinking about how she used to put sugar water on the top of her hand and honeybees would sip it, happily humming.

'Bees are a gardener's best friend,' she told me. 'No bees to pollinate the plants, no plums or raspberries. Would you like to try?' She nodded at the glass of sugar water.

I shook my head. I'm a little afraid of bees, ever since I stood on one in the garden when I was six. It stung the arch of my foot and I remember Mama pulling out the stinger with metal tweezers, rubbing honey onto my red, throbbing skin and wrapping a white bandage around it.

Mama always put honey on stings, cuts and bruises; she said it has magical healing properties. She rubbed it on her own skin so much she used to smell like honey, warm and sweet.

I wish I was as brave as Mama. I need to be brave right now.

Whack! Jonty is really going for it with that stick. I feel so sorry for my little brother. It's only been six months since Mama died and I know he's missing her dreadfully. We all are, although Papa rarely talks about her.

'Should I go after him, Papa? He's outside attacking the compost heap.' Jonty has started thrashing Mama's pile of old clippings and grass cuttings, sending a storm of tiny black dots into the air. Fruit flies. Jonty stands back, gently waving them away from his face. My brother literally wouldn't hurt a fly!

'No,' Papa says. 'Leave him outside.'

Papa's right. Jonty's like a wild animal – four walls cage him in. He loves being outside. I have no idea how he's going to cope in a small flat in the heart of Dublin city.

CHAPTER 2

A honeybee colony is made up of thousands of bees who are all
related to each other. They live together like one
very large family.

I'm going to miss our house, *Stella Maris*. It means 'Star of the Sea' in Latin. Mama told me that. Henrietta Street is nearer my art college – I looked it up in Mama's map book of Dublin – so at least that's something. I'll still get to see my friends.

I left school when Mama got sick to help look after her during the day. Papa enrolled me in art classes three nights a week instead at the Metropolitan School of Art. I was the youngest female student they'd ever accepted.

Mama wasn't keen on the idea of me leaving school, but I have my heart set on becoming an artist so Papa managed to talk her around. He's an artist himself, at least he was – a well-known illuminator and portrait painter, as well as a printer. Illuminators decorate things like speeches with fancy writing and illustrations, so you can frame them and put them on the wall. These days he can barely make out his hand in front of his face. He must miss painting. I know I'd be lost without my pencils and my sketchbooks.

I've lived in *Stella Maris* all my life. It's nothing grand like some of the houses in Rathmines – just a two-storey redbrick around a small square – but it's home. I wonder how long it will take for our new house to feel like home. Papa visited it alone, taking a jaunting car while Jonty was at school. I stayed at home, drawing a bowl of fruit for a college assignment.

As soon as he was inside the front door, I practically pounced on him. 'What's it like, Papa?' I asked. 'Henrietta Street?'

'Noisy,' he said, his voice a bit flat. 'I heard babies crying and boys shouting at each other. I think they were playing chasing. The hallway and the apartment smelt of carbolic soap.'

Then I realised, of course, what a stupid question! He couldn't *see* any of it.

'Carbolic soap,' I said brightly, helping him out of his coat and hanging it and his hat on the wooden coat stand. 'That's

good, isn't it, Papa? Means it's clean. And Jonty will love the chasing.' I wasn't so sure about the crying babies.

x x x

So we start packing up *Stella Maris* into wooden crates, our china wrapped in straw and old newspapers, our clothes carefully folded and draped into the boxes in layers. When I say 'we' it's mostly me and Sally.

Sally's our cook and housekeeper. We used to have a housemaid too, Maria, but when Papa's eyesight started to fade everything changed. And now we're facing the biggest change of all.

'Are you all right, mite?' Sally asks me as we wrap newspaper around the heavy Waterford crystal glasses from the dining-room cabinet. These crates have to be packed extra carefully as they are going to an auction house. Papa said we won't have the space for extra glasses and delft in Henrietta Street. 'You're fierce quiet.'

'I don't want to go. I'll miss you.' My voice wobbles a bit.

Sally hugs me and I breathe in her familiar smell – fresh baking and the strong peppermints she loves to suck. 'Ah, pet, it's not goodbye forever. I'll be working for Mr Pennefeather, you know, that nice friend of your father's; in a fancy house on Merrion Square, no less. It's not far from your new place, I'll make sure to come and see you when I can.'

'Promise?'

She dabs at my tears with the end of her apron. 'Promise.'

I don't know how we're going to cope without Sally, but Papa says we can't afford to pay her wages any more so we'll just have to.

Jonty spends most of our last week in *Stella Maris* in the garden, playing with Oboe and getting ready to say goodbye to him. If I'm quiet, Jonty's as silent as a mouse.

I take out my sketchbook and draw Oboe. I'm going to miss our loyal friend too.

X X X

The man who comes to take Oboe to Wicklow is kind, pretending not to see my brother's tears when he takes Oboe's lead from Jonty's hand. Oboe whines a bit and looks at Jonty, but the man rubs the fur under his fluffy chin and says, 'You're all right, boy,' settling him.

'I'll take good care of this fellow,' he promises Jonty who nods silently and then walks away, head low. I don't think he can bear to watch the jaunting car leave with Oboe sitting obediently up front beside his new master.

X X X

Papa closes his workshop on the Liffey quays for good –
Thomas Kane's Illumination and Printing Studio – and
manages to box up all his tools, paints and brushes largely by
touch, although I help.

Before Mama got sick, I used to spend a lot of time in
Papa's workshop. He showed me how to create an illumination from start to finish – how to plan and then pencil in the
design, how to mix all the inks and choose the right nibbed
pen for the lettering. It was always a happy, creative place and
I loved it. Like Jonty losing Oboe, I think closing the workshop and letting his staff go makes Papa's heart break a little.

All our belongings are loaded onto the back of a horse and
cart and our lives move from leafy Rathmines to our new
home, 16 Henrietta Street.

CHAPTER 3

Bees have an interesting life cycle. They grow from egg to larva, pupa to bee. The eggs are laid in hexagonal honeycomb cells made from bees' wax.

I sit in the left-hand seat of the jaunting car with Jonty beside me. Papa's on the right-hand side and the driver is up front, holding the horse's reins.

'Nearly there now,' I say to Jonty as we trundle over O'Connell Bridge and hit Sackville Street. I've only been up this grand street as far as the Gresham Hotel, with its fancy stone façade. I went there for afternoon tea with Mama before she got too sick to leave her bed. But I've been studying Mama's map book carefully, trying to get to know the area as well as I can.

Jonty ignores me, turning his head to study the shiny black horse pulling us along.

With every clip-clop of the horse's hooves we draw nearer and nearer Henrietta Street and I start to feel more and more nervous. I lean against the wooden backrest and close my eyes for a second. It's only ten in the morning and I've been up since six getting the last of the boxes packed with Sally. I'm exhausted. I could do without Jonty acting up.

I hear a sniff and spot him wiping away tears from his eyes.

'It's going to be all right, Jonty,' I say gently, my irritation melting.

We pass tea rooms and taverns, outfitters and milliners. Sackville Street is busy, the pavements crowded with ladies in feathered hats, gentlemen in smooth moleskin hats, ladies swinging large round hat boxes and clutching brown paper packages; bicycles, trams clanging their bells, jaunting cars and even the occasional motor car tooting its horn as it whizzes past. Papa had a smart black bicycle and he used to go everywhere on it before the problem with his eyes. Now it's been sold, along with Mama's bicycle and so many other things.

The smoggy air catches at the back of my throat. I cough a little and my eyes water. I'm starting to feel a bit over-whelmed. Rathmines village is busy – there are lots of shops and tea rooms – but it's nothing like this.

As we pass the Rotunda Hospital a gang of boys run in

front of the jaunting car, making the jarvey call out, 'Mind yerselves, for goodness sake!'

I watch as the boys run towards Rutland Square. I realise that only one of them is wearing boots. Could I run that fast in bare feet? I doubt it. I've seen boys without boots before – not in Rathmines, on my way in and out of college – but never so many of them together.

I stare down at my own brown laced boots with the small heel, an old pair of Mama's. I've kept lots of her clothes and shoes – she was very stylish and loved fashion. At first it made me too sad to wear them, but Sally said I was being silly. She said Mama was a very practical woman and would like her things to be re-used. 'Besides,' she said, 'She was some woman, your mother. She deserves to be remembered.'

Sally was right. Now I wear something of Mama's every day; it's like carrying a little bit of her with me.

X X X

We pass Rutland Square and turn right, onto Granby Row and then left onto Dorset Street. On Dorset Street I start to notice more and more women and children on the streets outside the Georgian houses. The place is teeming with life. Boys and girls playing on the pavements, mothers with babies on their hips chatting to each other, men leaning against the black railings in clumps.

The jaunting car slows down and turns sharp right into a street of tall four-storey houses all built on an incline, with a fine stone archway and big black gates at the top of the slope. I can see buildings behind the gates that look rather grand. My map book said it was King's Inns. I asked Papa and he said it's where lawyers are trained.

I think the houses were once red brick, but it's hard to tell now as they are streaked black as coal. Each building has stone steps leading up to the open front doors and fanlights; they must have been grand houses once upon a time but now most of the glass in the fanlights is broken and many of the windowpanes are spidered with cracks or missing completely and covered with boards.

We stop. 'Number sixteen Henrietta Street,' the jarvey says. It's the first house on the left-hand side.

The noise! The street is bedlam: children running up and down the muddy cobblestones, toddlers crawling and wobbling on the ground, some screaming crying. The group of women sitting on the steps of number fifteen all stop talking and stare at me. My stomach lurches. I look at Jonty.

His eyes are fixed on the gang of boys running down the hill, away from the large black gates yelling 'All in! All in! Free-all!' Like the boys I saw near the Rotunda, many of them are barefoot. Some of them are wearing women's jackets, and one of the younger ones is wearing a raggedy black girl's dress.

But all Jonty says is, 'I've always wanted to play Relievio. Do you think they'll let me join in?'

'Why don't you go and ask them?' I say. 'I'm sure they'll say yes.' I hope it's true. 'I'd better check with Papa first, though.'

I call over to Papa who is still sitting on far side of the jaunting car. 'Can Jonty go and play with some of the boys on the street?'

'Of course,' he says. 'Have fun, Jonty.'

'I will,' he says, jumping down from the seat and dashing towards the boys.

X X X

Our boxes have already been delivered to Henrietta Street so I swing down the small carpet bag I'd packed with some of our clothes and wash things and wait as Papa pays the driver.

I can feel the eyes of the women watching me and it makes my stomach knot up. As I stand at the bottom of the steps of number sixteen, a girl sticks her head out the open doorway. She's about my height and only a couple of years older than I am, fifteen maybe, but her eyes look like she's seen a lot of the world already. She looks at me curiously.

'Are you lost?' she asks in a strong Dublin accent. There's a bucket hooked over one arm and a scrubbing brush in her hand. Her black linen dress is old and worn, but the white apron over it is spotless and ironed to a crisp. Her black boots have string in place of laces, but are as clean as mine.

I shake my head.

'What are you after in there, so?' She nods her head into the lobby.

'We live here now.'

'Is that right?' Her eyes sweep up and down my high-collared white shirt, my emerald green skirt and jacket, my straw hat with the green ribbon.

'Off to Dublin Castle for a spot of afternoon tea with the King and Queen are you?'

I suddenly feel very overdressed. I do rather stand out in the sea of black, white and grey of the other girls' and women's clothes, like a green parrot in a flock of magpies and ravens. I can feel my cheeks go red.

A little boy with stick legs comes running towards her, one of his knees pouring blood. 'Annie, I'm after falling,' he says.

I'm not surprised, his boots are far too big for his feet.

She puts down her bucket and brush with a sigh. 'You poor thing.'

Walking past me she says, 'Ah here, don't mind me, green suits you. You look very smart. Welcome to Henrietta Street.'

'Thanks,' I say.

As she tends to the boy's knee, I notice Papa is standing beside me.

'Do you need a hand up the steps?' I ask him.

'I'll manage,' he says and we start walking up together.

He stands back to let me through the doorway. 'Ladies first.'

The first thing I notice is the stench. It smells like someone has used the hallway as a toilet, but that can't be right – who would do such a thing? – it must have been a cat or a dog.

In the dingy light I stare at the walls, the plaster painted a vivid red up to the handrail and a dull yellow over that. They are littered with all manner of dints and scrapes and some-one has carved their initials into the plaster with a knife, 'M.O'H'.

Everything is bare. Bare stone floor, bare wooden stairs,

bare walls – no pictures, hall table, nothing. This is our home now? I take a deep breath and try not to cry.

'We're on the very top floor,' Papa says. 'Bit of a climb I'm afraid.'

I swallow down the lump in my throat. 'That's all right, Papa. I'll just tell Jonty to follow us up. You go on ahead.'

I step back outside and take another deep breath. I need to make the most of things.

The girl – Annie – is staring up at me from the cobble-stones. There's fresh blood on her apron from the boy's knee.

We lock eyes for a second and this time she gives me a warm smile that makes me feel a bit better. At least some-one's friendly here.

I spot Jonty running down the hill at speed and shout at him, 'Jonty, we're on the top floor. Follow us up when you're ready.'

'I'll be ages,' he shouts back. 'George says it can go on for hours.' He comes closer and throws his jacket at me. His short trousers, knee socks and boots are already covered in mud, but he's grinning from ear to ear so I don't say anything.

'Come up when you get hungry,' I tell him. I'm glad he's happy and it will give me some time to get our flat ready. I hope it doesn't smell as bad as the hall. I cross my fingers and make a wish, please make it be clean.

Walking up the stairs I hear noises from behind some of the battered wooden doors of other flats, babies crying, a man talking loudly, what sounds like chair legs being scraped across floorboards.

It gets quieter towards the top of the house and the air gets better. As I reach the small top landing I smell carbolic soap. Papa is standing in front of a battered black door with a key in his hand.

I wait patiently as he feels the door for the lock and after a few attempts manages to get the key in and turn it.

I hold my breath and then I step inside.

CHAPTER 4

When a bee pupa has developed into a young bee, it chews its
way through the wax at the top of its honeycomb cell. Young
bees emerge from their honeycomb cells as either queens, female
worker bees or male drones.

'Eliza!' Jonty says, dashing through the door of our new flat. 'There's a stable outside with two ponies. And a shed with pigs. I'm not sure how many – it stank a bit – but I'll go back and count later. Papa didn't say anything about all the animals.'

'Shush, he's resting in bed, you'll wake him up.'

'Sorry.' He lowers his voice. 'George and Sid, that's his little brother, showed me around. Sid hurt his knee, but he was very brave about it. George is a real brick. Said I can play with them every day if I like.'

I've been sitting at the window in Papa's armchair wondering how on earth we're going to cope. The noise! The smell! The mud! But at least our flat is clean and bright and only a few of the windowpanes are broken. They've been covered with thin pieces of wood so the wind doesn't whistle in.

The window opens too, I discovered. When I first walked into the flat there was a bee sitting on the windowsill. I have no idea how it got there, but it waited patiently while I opened the window and gently whooshed it out with my hand.

Our floorboards are covered with our red and blue oriental rugs from home, making the floors much cosier. Papa asked the removal men to put up some of Mama's favourite pictures, landscapes painted by the art teacher in the school she used to work in, Alexandra College. Mama was the French teacher there. I went there too, before leaving for art college.

I'm trying to stay positive, but our flat is tiny. It's a flat for mice! There are three small spaces that have been carved out of one attic room with wooden partitions that don't even fully reach the sloped ceiling. One space has a brass bed for Papa, another has two narrow beds against the walls, one for me and one for Jonty. The room I'm sitting in is long and narrow, with a window overlooking the street and a small fireplace. It will have to be the 'everything room' – sitting room, dining room *and* kitchen.

I give Jonty my best attempt at a smile. 'We're going to be all right here, you'll see.' I hope it's true. I think of the girl outside and her kind smile and hold it in my heart; it gives me hope.

X X X

The following morning – Saturday – I manage to cook some porridge in a pot on the fire, the way Sally taught me – oatmeal and water with a dollop of honey once it's cooked to sweeten it.

She gave me a small black notebook full of recipes that she'd copied out for me. It must have taken her ages – she's not a fast writer. I'd been helping her in the kitchen since Mama died, so cooking for Papa and Jonty from now on isn't too scary. And at least we have our own tap and sink in the workshop so we don't have to share the one in the busy yard. The less I think about the yard and the closets right now the better.

I went downstairs to use one of the closets in the twilight last night – Papa told me they were in the yard out the back – big mistake! Going down the stairway was terrifying; it was full of dark shadows and strange scratching noises. I had a lamp with me, but it didn't make it any easier. And when I spotted the closets and opened the door of the nearest one, I nearly passed out. It was so stinky and revolting I turned on my heels and ran all the way back up the stairs.

Luckily we have chamber pots so I was able to use one of those instead. I put one under Papa and Jonty's beds too, just in case.

After that I didn't sleep well. I kept hearing noises: a baby crying in one of the flats below us, someone climbing the stairs and singing to himself, and horrible scuttling under the floorboards. We had field mice in our house in Rathmines before, but this didn't sound like mice. It's not rats, I kept telling myself. It's definitely not rats.

This morning I had the lovely job of emptying the chamber pots into a metal slop bucket and going downstairs to throw it into one of the closets. I had to hold my breath when I went inside. The stench in there was worse than the piggery and that's saying something.

The yard itself is big with muddy cobblestones. There are washing lines strung across it and an archway out to the laneway at the back; Henrietta Cottages, the sign said.

I had a quick walk down the laneway, which was pretty narrow and mucky. Some of the houses are small cottages with muddy white walls, but at the far end of the laneway, the King's Inns end, the houses are taller, two and three storeys. It's a real mishmash. The air down there is dank and some of the buildings look as if they are just about standing. Our flat may be small, but at least it's bright and has solid walls.

Like Henrietta Street, the laneway was full of children, only they were much dirtier. Some of them streeled after me, asking me for money, which made me feel awkward.

'Give us a farthing, miss, go on.'

They didn't follow me back into the yard, thank goodness.

Jonty wolfs down his porridge, but Papa eats only a few spoonfuls.

'It's not as good as Sally's, Papa, but I tried,' I say. I go to take his bowl and he reaches out for my hand and holds it, his palm cool against my skin.

'Eliza, you're the best daughter ever. And you've done wonders with our new home. I know it's small, but at least we're all together. Your mother would be so proud, poppet.'

I'm surprised. It's the first time he's mentioned Mama in ages. 'Thank you, Papa.'

'Now, let's get down to business,' he says, rubbing his hands together.

I smile to myself. Now he's sounding more like the old Papa. Full of plans and ideas.

'Today is the first day of our new lives,' he says. 'Things are going to have to change. I'm still getting enquiries about illuminations, which is good but obviously I can't work on them at the moment, so I've made a decision. Eliza, you've watched me do them for years now, I think you're ready to try it for yourself. It will keep some money coming in so we don't have to use up all our savings.'

'What about art college?' My heart beats faster in my chest. I love my classes. The tutors say I have talent, but I need to practise.

'You'll have to leave,' he says. 'For the time being anyway.'

'But Papa, can't I do both?'

'We can't afford your college fees. The rent on this place is five shillings a week and then there's fuel and food on top of that.'

I look around; surely it can't be that expensive for this place? It's hardly the lap of luxury!

'I'll also need you to get Jonty up and take him to school in the mornings,' he adds. 'He can make his own way home.'

'Why does he get to go to school?' I say. 'He doesn't even

like school. It's not fair!'

'She's right,' Jonty says. 'Can't stand it. I'm going to live in Wicklow when I grow up and have as many dogs as I like. Hundreds of 'em. All that reading and writing malarkey is wasted on me.' He looks at Papa. 'Hang on, how am I going to school in Rathmines from here? On the tram?' His eyes sparkle: Jonty loves the tram.

'No,' Papa says. 'Your old school is too far away, and we can't afford the tram every day, from now on it's only for special occasions. Apparently, the schools around here are very crowded. The Pennefeathers have an excellent tutor for their boys and have kindly said you can join them, Jonty. You start on Monday.'

'Rats!' Jonty says. 'Do I have to?'

'Yes,' Papa says firmly.

I remember that Sally is working for the Pennefeathers, which softens the blow a little. At least I might get to see her every day.

'Fine,' I say. 'I'll bring him to the Pennefeathers every morning. Can we take the tram on Monday, Papa? Seeing as it's his first day?'

'All right then,' Papa says. 'A special first-day treat.'

Jonty perks up a bit at this. 'Fine, I'll go. But I don't need any of that education stuff. I ain't going to be a lawyer or a banker, mind. Bor-ing!'

'Why are you talking like that?' I ask.

'Like what?'

I was about to say like a street boy, but I stop myself. It's what one of my teachers used to say when we forgot our grammar. 'With a weird accent,' I say instead.

'I have to change how I talk,' Jonty says. 'And quick. George calls me a toff as it is and he likes me. The others ain't as kind. Aren't, I mean.'

'Well, you can't talk like that at the Pennefeathers or in front of Papa,' I say.

Jonty sticks out his tongue at me. 'Goody Two Shoes. I'll talk how I like.'

'Stop squabbling, you two,' Papa says. 'It's exhausting. But your sister does have a point, Jonty. Best behaviour at the Pennefeathers and try to talk like a young gentleman. Now, Eliza, will you buy me a newspaper please? You can read it to me so I can find out what's going on in the world. I know the paper is a bit of a luxury, but I'll only get it on Saturdays to economise.'

'Of course, Papa. I'll get some milk and bread while I'm out. And something for dinner. I'll take Jonty with me. It'll be an adventure.'

Papa hands me three pennies. I have no idea how much milk and bread cost, but I hope it's enough. 'Some adventure,' Jonty grumbles. 'We're hardly going to bump into any pirates or cowboys out getting milk.'

'You never know, Jonty,' I say. 'Keep your eyes peeled.'

Papa smiles, something else he hasn't done in a long time. 'See you later, my little explorers.'

CHAPTER 5

Each colony has several hundred drones. Male drones have no sting. Their only job is to fertilise the queen, helping to create thousands of new bees.

Jonty dashes down the stairs ahead of me and I run after him. He's not looking where he's going and almost trips over a woman who is scrubbing the stairs. Luckily I manage to grab his arm just in time to swing him away from her. But we give her a right fright.

'Hey!' she says loudly, dropping her scrubbing brush onto the steps with a clatter.

'Is for horses.' Did I just say that out loud? Oops! Me and my big mouth.

She straightens up and looks at me. I can feel my cheeks go redder and redder as she stares. It's not a woman at all, it's the girl who asked was I off for afternoon tea with the King and Queen. Then to my huge relief her face breaks into a smile.

'My mam used to say that,' she says. 'Hay is for horses. Always made me laugh.'

'My Mama did too,' I say.

She scoots her body around so her back is resting against the wall, stretches the fingers of her scrubbing hand in and out a few times and gives a happy sigh. 'So you moved in all right?'

'Yes, thank you,' I say.

She nods. 'What are your names then?'

'I'm Eliza Kane and the human whirlwind is my brother, Jonty.'

'Sorry about that,' Jonty mumbles.

'S'all right.' She pushes her hair back from her flushed face. 'Annie O'Hanlon's the name, scrubbin's the game. Today at least. I do my best to keep the floors and the stairs clean. You lot are all right on the la-di-da upper flat. Only three of you in that huge place. And a workshop to boot. Talk about nobby luxury.' Then she stops. 'Sorry, mouth running away with me.' She smiles at me again.

I smile back. 'How many live in your flat?'

'Usually eight, but our lodger's just moved out, thank goodness. So one room, seven bodies. Not much fun. But we're lucky, at least it's just us lot. Some families have to share with others. There are ten families in this building, all in all.'

Ten families in one house? And seven people in one room? I try not to look too shocked. It must be a huge room to take so many beds.

'Any boys my age?' Jonty says.

Annie cocks her head. 'What are you, thirteen?'

He grins. 'Ten.' It's kind of her as Jonty's on the small side for his age. I sometimes wonder if that's why he acts younger than he is. That and the fact that Mama babied him for years. He was her little pet.

'In that case, yes,' she says. 'And I think you've already met them. George is eleven and Sid's nine.'

'They're your brothers?'

'They are. And I have three older brothers, but you won't see much of 'em, they work at the docks with my da, when he's able.'

'George and Sid are bricky!' Jonty says. 'How is Sid's knee?'

She smiles. 'All clean and bandaged up like a soldier's.'

I think about this for a second. The boy with the cut knee is nine? He looked about six.

'They're on the street playing if you want to join them,' she says.

Jonty looks at me. 'Can I?'

'When we come back from shopping,' I say. 'Maybe you can help us, Annie. Where are the shops?'

Annie tilts her head. 'What are you after exactly? Veg? Coal?'

'*The Freeman's Journal* for my father, milk and bread. And maybe some meat.'

Annie nods. 'Varian Brothers at the top of Sackville Street will see you right. Bit of everything in there. Meat? Special occasion is it?'

'Not really,' I say. 'Why, is meat expensive?'

'Can be. On a budget are you?' She gives a laugh. 'Why am I asking? You're living here, ain't you? Bit different to what you're used to I'd say, judging by your clothes and the way you speak. Hope you don't mind me saying. No offence, like.' She gives me a grin.

I smile back. She's right, it's not what we're used to. 'None taken,' I say. 'And yes, we are on a budget. Very much so.'

She nods again. 'Ask for meat parings, they're nice and cheap. You should get enough to make a decent stew along with some potatoes and veg for a penny. Don't let them charge you more than two pennies, mind.'

'Thanks, Annie,' I say. 'That's really helpful.'

'Be seeing you, Eliza.' Annie grins again. 'Many times a day. You're one of us now, the big Henrietta Street family. We watch out for each other so let me know if you need anything, you hear. Mind where you're steppin' in future, Jonty. And careful of the rats at night. Big as dogs they are.'

X X X

As we walk towards Sackville Street, Jonty says 'I thought I heard something under the floorboards last night. Do you think it was a giant rat like Annie said?'

'No!' I insist. 'Absolutely not! There are no rats in this building.'

But he keeps at it. 'Do you think they really are as big as dogs? What kind of dogs do you think? Little terriers or great big wolfhounds?'

'Yuck, Jonty, stop! You're giving me the shivers. You know I hate them.' I really can feel my skin crawl.

'I'll ask George and Sid. I bet they know all about the rats and interesting stuff like that.'

CHAPTER 6

A honeybee in flight can beat its wings over one
hundred times a second.

On Monday morning we wait at the stop on the top of Sackville Street for the tram to whizz us to the Pennefeathers. It took a lot of energy to get Jonty ready, and I didn't sleep a wink last night, worrying about all kinds of things like Papa's eyesight and how we're going to survive on vegetables and meat parings. Even thought it was edible, it didn't taste of much and Jonty wasn't impressed.

'Is this all there is?' he said. 'Soup with lumps in it?' He lifted up a piece of meat with his spoon and stared at it. 'What is this? Beef or mutton? Or rat?'

'Just eat it, Jonty,' I said. 'You can fill up with bread and butter.'

I'm not even sure we can afford butter every day from now on. It cost a penny in the shop for a small pat and a bag of coal was two whole shillings. Which I now know is a fortune! I hadn't paid much attention to how much things cost before, but at the moment it's all I can think of.

'Why do I have to go to school?' he moaned as I made him wash his face over the washbasin. 'And this water's freezing.'

'You know why and stop complaining.' I was tired and in no mood for his nonsense.

He kicked the base of the washstand and gave a yelp. 'Me toe. I've hurt me toe.'

'*My* toe and shush, you'll wake up Papa. Don't be such a baby.'

'*You're* a baby.'

'Jonty, we don't have time for this. Stop acting the maggot and get on with it.'

At the tram stop Jonty kicks at a stone – his toe has miraculously healed – and I'm about to take out my sketchbook to draw him when I spot a long, crimson poster stuck to the lamp post.

MR ZOZIMUS WILDE'S FAMOUS TRAVELLING CIRCUS

BLACK CHURCH SQUARE, DUBLIN

3RD JUNE TO 24TH JUNE

PRESENTING: MR ZOZIMUS WILDE AND HIS

REMARKABLE DANCING HORSES

(WILL MR WILDE DARE TO RIDE

ON THEIR BARE BACKS?)

MISS KARINA ZEMKOVA, THE LION QUEEN

(WILL SHE TAME THOSE FEROCIOUS BEASTS?)

MADAM ADA WILDE, FAMOUS BEE CHARMER AND HER

REMARKABLE SWARMS

(YOU WILL NOT BELIEVE YOUR EYES!)

THE AFRICAN PRINCESS, MISS LULU

THE HUMAN BUTTERFLY

MISS COCO THE LADY CLOWN, THE FLYING FANZINIS

AND OUR MAGICAL PERFORMING DOGS

AND MUCH MORE! ROLL UP, ROLL UP! EVERYONE LOVES

MR ZOZIMUS WILDE'S FAMOUS TRAVELLING CIRCUS!

'Jonty, look!' I point at the poster.

He stops kicking and starts to read, his eyes growing wider and wider. 'Eliza, it says they have lions. And dancing horses. And dogs! We have to go.'

'I'll ask Papa,' I say. I know money is tight at the moment but there's a chance he'll say yes if I catch him in the right mood and I don't want to crush Jonty's spirit. Especially as the poster seems to have cheered him out of his 'going to school' grump. We're lucky the Pennefeathers are being so kind. From the amount of children around Jonty's age on Henrietta Street this morning it doesn't look like many of them make it to school every day, or at all. Although I'm not surprised, Mr Pennefeather is a really nice man.

He's an artist, like Papa. His family appears to have pots of money so he doesn't seem to have to work much in the book-shop he owns, he just paints. I've always loved the bright purple and crimson cravats he wears and his embroidered waistcoats. Mama used to say he was a 'true eccentric'.

He has a bushy white beard and is always smiling. He and Papa used to go to Gaelic League meetings together every week when we lived in Rathmines. Mr Pennefeather would arrive at the door to collect Papa in his shiny black Benz

Velo motor car and pass Papa a pair of funny-looking driving goggles to put on.

One evening I overheard him say to Papa in the hall as they got ready to go: 'Florence will have nothing to do with my driving. She says my motor car's a dangerous monster of a contraption and I'm going to kill us both.' Florence is Mrs Pennefeather, his wife. I've never met her – Mr Pennefeather always visited Papa alone.

Papa just laughed and said 'Lead on, MacDuff', which is from one of Mr Shakespeare's plays. Papa is a big Shakespeare fan. He was in an amateur dramatics society in Rathmines with Mr Pennefeather before Mama died, and he played Hamlet and Macbeth. I can't remember the last time he broke into one of Mr Shakespeare's speeches or even quoted him.

A few weeks after Mama died, Mr Pennefeather took me and Jonty for a ride around Rathmines and as far as Rathgar in his motor car. I think he was trying to cheer us up. It zoomed along, much faster than a horse and carriage. Noisier too – the chug-chug of the engine made it hard to hear anything or talk.

I was scared silly at first but once we started moving it

was great fun. Everyone stared at us and some people even clapped and cheered. Mr Pennefeather said there are not too many motor cars in Ireland so it might have been the finest one they'd ever seen in Rathmines.

Recently Papa has stopped going to his Gaelic League meetings. I asked him about it and he says he doesn't want people to know how bad his eyesight is now. If they know the truth they will stop sending him work. And then we'll be in real trouble. I hadn't realised he was going to pass off my illumination work as his own – now I feel extra pressure to do it well! Starting today.

I hear the loud whirr of the tram as it trundles towards us and then stops with a screech. The burning-rubber smell of the brake pads tickles my nose. The sign on it says 'Dalkey via Merrion Square' and there's a large green shamrock too. Papa said to look out for the shamrock, then we'd know we were on the right tram.

'This is us. Ready?' I ask Jonty.

'Too right!'

He swings himself onto the tram using the shiny rail. Even though it's windy, he whips up the narrow stairs to the top deck while I pay the conductor.

'Jonty, be careful,' I say as he stumbles a bit. 'You're going too fast.' But he ignores me.

The conductor laughs. 'Bit excited is he?'

I smile. 'How did you guess?'

I climb the stairs carefully after Jonty, my hand clutching the rail. Staying upright when the tram is moving is no joke as it swaggers and sways a bit as it moves along, like a ship on the high seas. I find Jonty in the very front seat, holding the brass bar in front of him, a huge grin on his face. I sit down beside him.

'Isn't this brilliant, Eliza?' he says. 'Whizzo! We can see everything from up here. There's Nelson's Pillar.'

I look over at it. There are seagulls sitting on the statue's shoulders and a large one on Nelson's head. I nudge Jonty with my shoulder. 'Look at the seagulls.'

He leans in towards me, lowering his voice. 'Looks like that big one is doing a dropping on Nelson's hair.'

I laugh. I know Jonty's sad about leaving Oboe and Rathmines so I'm glad he's enjoying himself. He may be annoying a lot of the time but he's the only brother I've got.

As we head towards O'Connell Bridge, I take out my sketchbook and start drawing Jonty: the excitement on his face, the wind catching his mop of curly blond hair. Mama's hair. Mine's poker straight and dark, dark brown, almost black. Mama used to plait it for me every morning, her plaits were always perfect. Now I have to do it myself. I miss Mama. I take a deep breath and try to concentrate on my drawing.

I draw a seagull next, then a whole flock of them. Next thing I know the conductor's calling 'Merrion Square. All out for Merrion Square' and I jump up.

'This is our stop, Jonty. Quick!' We scramble down the stairs and jump off the tram just in time.

X X X

We find the Pennefeathers' house easily. It's hard to miss the huge four-storey redbrick.

Jonty stares up at it and whistles. 'The Pennefeathers must be really rich,' he says. 'Millionaires or something.'

'Shush, Jonty! Best behaviour, remember? You don't want to get kicked out of school on your first day.'

His eyes light up and I can see I've given him an idea. A terrible idea. If he thinks it will get him out of going to school there's no end to the horrors he might cook up for the Pennefeathers' tutor.

'Jonty, no!' I say quickly. 'Papa would be so disappointed if you act up today.' Then I have a thought. 'And we'll never get to the circus if he's cross with you.'

He sighs. 'That would be tragic. All right, I'll be a good little doggie.' He sticks out his tongue and pants like a puppy, making me laugh.

'Come here.' His hair is a mess and I reach out to smooth it down with my fingers but he whips his head away.

'I suppose you'll have to do,' I say. I walk up the granite

steps to the grand oxide-red front door and give a knock with the shiny brass lion's head. Jonty has gone quiet and I can tell he's doing his best to stay still.

I hear steps coming towards the door. 'You all right?' I ask him.

He nods, looking a little pale. The heavy door swings slowly open.

CHAPTER 7

There are thousands of species or different kinds of bees in the world and each one is different.

A tall man in a dark three-piece suit looks at me and then at Jonty.

'You must be Master and Miss Kane. Madam has been expecting you. Please come in.'

We step inside and he closes the door behind us. There are black and white marble tiles on the floor and a huge chandelier hanging over our heads. I've never seen anything like it! The crystal droplets are catching the rays of sun shining through the fanlight and sending splinters of coloured light across the walls. I even spot a tiny rainbow dancing on the ceiling.

Mama explained that rainbows happen when glass, or in this case crystal, splits light into different colours. Rain can do the same outside – split the light – creating rainbows in the sky. I try not to stare, but the chandelier is so beautiful.

I've been in Papa and Mama's friends' houses before, but none of them were as grand as this one; it's practically a palace.

There's a vase of pink roses on the marble hall table and I breathe in the sweet scent. I try not to think of the lobby at Henrietta Street and its smell.

'This way, please.' The man starts to walk briskly towards the white marble staircase.

He sounds and looks so formal with his suit and neatly oiled hair that I'm finding it hard not to giggle. I know looking at Jonty – who is bound to pull a face at me or wiggle his eyebrows – would set me off so I focus on the man's poker-straight back as we follow him down the hallway and up a flight of stairs.

He stops in front of a door to the right of the landing and gives a sharp rap on the wood with his knuckle.

'Enter,' comes a high-pitched voice from inside. He shows us in.

'Master and Miss Kane, Madam,' he says, giving the woman sitting on the gold brocade sofa a small bow.

'Thank you, Dalton,' she says, closing the book on her knee and placing it on the sofa beside her. I have a look at the spine. It's called *A Room with a View* by E. M. Forster.

She then flutters her fingers at Mr Dalton. It seems to be her way of telling him to leave.

'Very good, Madam.' He nods and closes the door behind himself.

The woman is staring directly at me so I look back at her. Her eyes are a strange colour – hazel, like cat's eyes. She has high cheekbones and she's wearing a white lace blouse with cloud-sized puffy sleeves and a high collar, tucked into a black taffeta skirt. The shiny silver buckle on her belt has a peacock's head on it.

Her big cat eyes are making me nervous.

'So, you are the Kane children,' she says. 'Your father is keeping well, I hope?'

'Very well, thank you, Mrs Pennefeather,' I say.

'Call me Madam,' she corrects me. 'I was sorry to hear about your mother from Mr Pennefeather. Tragic in one so young. Consumption is a dreadful illness. Highly infectious too.'

Then she turns her gaze to Jonty. 'Mr Pennefeather insists that you join my sons' lessons. John, isn't it?'

Jonty winces. He hates his real name. I press my foot against his to warn him to be polite, but it's no use.

'Jonty,' he says. 'I don't like John.'

Mrs Pennefeather's eyebrows lift. 'Is that right? My Harold and Theodore are just the same. It's Harry this and Theo that. But in my house and to my boys you will be John, understand? Jonty sounds like a name you'd give a pet pony or a dog.'

I press my foot against his again and this time he gets the message. Not that having a dog or pony's name would bother him in the slightest.

'Yes, Madam,' he says, making his voice as posh and formal as Mr Dalton's. 'I quite understand.' I try not to laugh. Luckily Mrs Pennefeather doesn't seem to notice.

'Mr Pennefeather tells me that you've just moved to Henrietta Street,' she says. 'So you must forgive me if I put a few precautions in place. I believe there are as many as four families living in one house this size. Can't be sanitary. All that mud in the streets and even rats, I've heard.'

I don't like to tell her that according to Annie there are ten families in our building. Or that it looks nothing like this building, not any more! And Jonty keeps his mouth shut too, thank goodness. Even about the rats. He can be smart when he wants to.

'In the morning you will deliver your brother to the servants' entrance in the basement, Miss Kane,' she says. 'And he will leave through the same entrance after his high tea with the boys at half-past five. I'm sure you'd prefer to feed him at home, but once again Mr Pennefeather insists.'

'Thank you,' I say. 'That's very kind of you. I'm sure Jonty, I mean John, appreciates it, don't you?'

'Yes,' he says. 'Eliza's a rubbish cook.'

'You must miss Sally,' Mrs Pennefeather says. 'Although I must say she is a rather plain cook. I've had to find her some French recipe books to freshen up her menus. Luckily Mr Pennefeather has plenty of access to books.' She gives a tinkling laugh. Mr Pennefeather's bookshop on the quays is a treasure trove. Mama and Papa used to take us there every Christmas to choose new books as a special treat.

'Do you like books, Madam?' I ask, genuinely interested. There's a glass-fronted bookshelf in the room stuffed with leather-bound books.

'Yes, they are one of life's great pleasures, don't you think? And there's so much to be learned from reading. And speaking of books, John, yours will be kept in the study and only in the study. You will not take them home, understand? I have instructed your tutor, Mr Stephens, to make sure this happens.'

Jonty smiles at this. 'So no homework then?'

'No, all your work will be done here. And you will also wear a uniform while you are under our roof. Arrive in your own clothes and you will change in the butler's office every morning before class. And make sure your hands and nails are scrubbed clean. Is all that clear? Cleanliness is so important to good health.'

She's looking at Jonty so he nods and says, 'Yes, Madam. Crystal clear.'

But I'm fuming inside. I've worked out exactly why Jonty can't take his books home and has to wear special 'Merrion Square' clothes and scrub his hands and nails – she's afraid her precious children will catch something off him. That fleas will hop from his breeches onto one of her sons!

I'm so angry I feel like telling *her* to hop it, but I know I can't. Jonty needs to get an education. But maybe there's a local school that isn't too crowded he could go to instead, far away from this horrible woman. I must ask Annie later. For now he'll have to put up with Madam and her 'precautions'.

'You are dismissed,' Mrs Pennefeather says.

'Thank you so much, Madam,' Jonty says, bowing so low his head almost touches the ground. 'You really are the most beautiful woman in Dublin. Everyone says so and it's true. Your eyes are like diamonds.'

Jonty! He's done it now. I hold my breath. But she seems to think he's being serious and gives another tinkling laugh. 'Why, you are a tonic, John. I think you'll fit in here just wonderfully.'

She pulls a wooden knob set into the wall beside her and seconds later Dalton appears.

'Miss Kane is leaving now,' she tells him. 'Please see her out and bring Master Kane downstairs to put on his new uniform. And don't forget to check for you know what.'

She touches her hair and he nods. 'Of course, Madam.'

Nits! She's suggesting that Jonty has nits! How dare she? Horrid woman!

As we walk down the stairs behind Mr Dalton I try not to let Jonty see how annoyed I am.

I say in a low voice, 'Sorry about all the uniform stuff. But it will keep your own clothes clean. And at least you'll get a good feed after studying. Sally will see to that.'

He grins at me. 'I'll be fine, don't worry. Papa told me to say that about her being a great beauty. He said it would soften her up. Worked too. Beauty my eye, she's an old witch.'

Mr Dalton stumbles on the stairs and grabs onto the polished wooden stair rail.

'Are you all right, Mr Dalton?' I ask him.

'Quite all right,' he says. But his lips are pressed together tightly, like he's trying not to laugh and his eyes have softened.

He leans towards me. 'We'll take care of your brother, don't you worry, Miss. And Madam's not all bad. She has a good heart underneath all of them airs and graces.' His voice is different now, warm, with a Dublin accent like Annie's. 'I'm from Rutland Street,' he adds. 'Us tenement kids have to stick together.'

CHAPTER 8

The honeybee belongs to the Apidae *family, along with the bumblebee. Bees in the* Apidae *family tend to have stout bodies and lots of hair.*

Before walking back to Henrietta Street, I sit on the bottom step of the Pennefeathers' house and take out my sketchbook. Drawing always calms me down. I draw Mrs Pennefeather – 'Madam' – with an extra-long beaky nose, a pointy chin and a big hairy wart on her cheek. I put her riding on a broomstick, all alone. No black cat to keep her company. She doesn't deserve a friend.

I start to draw tiny fleas hopping all over her. I draw more and more until they engulf her in a swirling black swarm. Until crack! The lead of my pencil snaps and I have to stop.

X X X

When I get back to our flat, Papa is sitting in his armchair with his eyes closed.

I put my hand on his arm. 'Papa, it's me. Are you asleep?'

'No child, just resting.' He opens his eyes and sits up straighter. 'So how did it go? Did Jonty behave himself with Mrs Pennefeather? Or did she behave with him, I should say. She can be a little…' He pauses for second. 'Tricky. I think she's bored, to be honest. Very bright woman. Always reading. She was training to be a nurse at the Adelaide when Mr Pennefeather first met her. Left to marry him and run the house.'

I pull over a dining chair and sit in front of him, so he has some chance of seeing me. Poor Papa, his eyes are looking even cloudier than usual today. 'Jonty's no fool,' I say. 'He's well able for her. He told her she was beautiful and after that she was all smiles.'

Papa laughs. 'Ha! I knew that would work. And she really was a great beauty in her day, full of spirit too, until she forgot how to smile. Poor Cedric. But as you say, Jonty will be just fine.' Cedric is Mr Pennefeather.

I don't tell him about the uniform or the nit checking. Papa seems in a good mood and I don't want to knock him out of it.

'So to business,' Papa says, rubbing his hands together. 'The Dublin Merchants Association wants to present Alderman

Tom Kelly with a framed letter thanking him for his work. They want it to look like a page from the Book of Kells, done on real vellum, with lots of Celtic animals and Celtic knots. I have the design worked out in my head. I just need you to draw it and colour it in. Can you do that, Eliza? All by yourself?'

'Vellum? That's unusual, but I'll do my best.'

'Good. They've paid me half up front and it will see us right for the next few weeks.' If that's the case, maybe now is a good time to ask him about the circus.

'Papa, on our way to the Pennefeathers we spotted a poster for the circus. It's only two pence each in the afternoons for children. Jonty would love to go and it would really cheer him up.'

Papa goes quiet for a moment. 'Eliza, I don't want to burden you with our finances, but unless things change and my eyesight improves we can't afford extra things like that. Or any more tram rides. I'm sorry.'

I take a deep breath and ask the question I've been dying to ask for ages now but haven't dared. 'Do you think your eyes *are* getting any better?'

He shakes his head. 'No. They're still blurry. I've seen a

doctor that Mr Pennefeather knows. There's an operation, but it's risky and very expensive. Almost five pounds and we don't have that kind of money to spare. And if it failed I could be completely blind. At least I can still see a bit. Enough to know your face has gone all serious, Eliza.' He reaches out and pats my hand. 'Please try not to worry. Mr Pennefeather is kindly taking orders for work for me in his bookshop. I've told him only to accept one a week so you're not under too much strain, my dear.'

'Thank you, Papa.' But he's just admitted that our whole family's survival depends on me. Me! It's just as well he can't see my face properly or he'd realise how worried I am. My heart is thumping in my chest and I need air. I have to get out of here.

I jump to my feet. 'Papa, I'm just going to fetch some paper and a fresh pencil from the workshop. We can start planning the Alderman's letter then.'

I race down the stairs and this time it's me who nearly takes Annie out. She's walking out of her flat and presses herself up against the wall so we don't collide.

'Slow down there, Eliza. You're in a rush. Where are you off to then? You look a bit pink, you all right?'

'Do you ever feel like screaming, Annie?'

She gives a laugh. 'Only every bloomin' day. I'm on my way to my charring job and I can't be late, but walk with me if you have time. Get what's bothering you off your chest.'

We start making our way down the stairs together. It's wide enough that we can walk side by side and having her close is making me feel a little calmer already.

'You clean houses?' I ask. 'Does it pay well?'

'It's not bad. Every house pays me nine pence a week. And I take in washing too. I make another half a shilling a week doing that.'

'Good for you,' I say, meaning it. Although it sounds like a lot of work for the money. She can't earn more than a couple of shillings a week. I just spent two whole pennies on a tram ride for me and Jonty!

As we walk down the stairs and out the door, I tell Annie about Papa and his eyes and how I have to take over his work and how worried I am about keeping everything going.

She listens carefully.

'What did you do before your father got sick?' she asks. 'I bet you were a shop girl. You're clever enough to be a shop girl.'

'I was in art college,' I say. 'I really miss all my friends there.'

'Art college?' Annie gasps. 'No! You don't say? I've never met a college girl. Or an artist. You must be dead talented. I'd love to see some of your stuff. I'm sorry you miss your friends, but I'll be your friend if you'll have me.'

I smile. 'I'd love that.'

X X X

At the corner of Henrietta Street and Bolton Street there's a crowd of children gathered around a lamp post. I follow their gazes. Sitting on the lamp, mewing loudly, is a jet-black cat.

'Daft moggy,' Annie says. 'Gets stuck up there every week, regular as clockwork.'

As we watch, a tall dark-haired boy calls up to him, 'Raven, come on Raven. You know how to get down. Up towards the curly bit and then down the post.' He starts climbing the lamp post, his long arms and legs making short work of it.

'And even dafter lad,' Annie says. She raises her voice. 'Joseph McAllister, you're going to hurt yourself.' He's a fast climber and is almost halfway up the lamp post by this stage.

He looks down and waves. 'Annie, my favourite girl. How are you?'

'Get down from there, you eejit,' she says. 'Use your noggin. Go find a ladder.'

But he's almost at the cat now, who jumps onto his shoulder.

For goodness' sake,' Annie says, 'you're going to kill yourself one of these days.'

Joseph climbs back down, and before reaching the bottom, takes a jump and lands back on the pavement in front of us. The children cheer and chant, 'Tall Joe, Tall Joe, Tall Joe!' I see why they call him that: he's a beanpole, at least six foot five, maybe even taller.

He walks towards us, cat now cradled in his arm, gives a flourish with one hand and drops into a bow in front of

Annie, his curly mop of black hair falling over his face and blocking out his unusual green eyes. 'M'Lady. May I have the honour of the second dance? The first must go to the beautiful Lady Raven.' He starts to waltz with the cat in his arms, as the children around him hoot with laughter.

Annie smiles and rolls her eyes. 'You're daft as a brush, Joseph McAllister. And I'm late. Can't stand here gabbing.'

'I'll walk with you,' he says eagerly. 'Just give me a second, need to collect the new table leg.' He puts the cat inside his shirt and then picks up a large piece of iron, which is resting against the railings.

'Where did you get that?' Annie asks.

'Docks. It's an old piece of railway track they were dumping. Ma likes dancing on the table so I need to make all the legs stronger.'

Annie laughs. 'Really?'

He grins. 'Nah, the weight of her sewing machine did them in. Spindly old things to begin with. Four of these will see it right.' He pats the railway track. 'Won't be the height of elegance, but it will do the trick. Who's your new friend, Annie? And where are you off to?'

'Eliza Kane. And that's for me to know and you to find

out.' She laughs, grabbing my arm and pulling me away. We march down the road together, arm in arm.

When we reach Dorset Street, I ask her 'Who was that?'

'Neighbour. Joseph McAllister. Tall Joe to most. Lives in Henrietta Cottages with his Mam and little brother and sister.' From the way her eyes light up when she talks about him, I think there's a story there.

A new friend and a mystery boy all in one day – I'm starting to think maybe living on Henrietta Street isn't going to be so bad after all.

CHAPTER 9

The smallest bee in the world is the Perdita Minima *and is smaller than an ant.*

Surprisingly Jonty's up before me on Tuesday morning. I can hear him moving around our room, grabbing his clothes and putting them on. I stay in bed, inching out a few more minutes before I have to get up. It's warm and cosy under my quilt and blankets, my own little cocoon.

'Eliza,' he says. 'Rise and shine, lazy bones. Time to smile at the day.' It was one of Mama's sayings and hearing it makes my heart squeeze.

I open my eyes and give a big yawn. 'Morning, Jonty. What's got you up so sparky then?'

'Sally said if I get to the Pennefeathers' before nine she'll give me a full cooked breakfast. Sausages and everything.'

'Did she now? That's kind of her.' My stomach grumbles. We are almost out of porridge oats and I'll have to give the last of them to Papa. 'We'd better hurry up in that case.'

I've never known what it's like to be hungry before. Papa says we have to keep to a budget of nine shillings and eight pence a week for food and that won't go far! We can have meat only twice a week, the other days it will have to be a soup made with cabbage and potatoes, and bread to mop it up. It's not enough for Jonty who eats like a horse so Sally's offer is a precious gift.

X X X

We practically sprint the whole way to the Pennefeathers' house – down Sackville Street (I'd forgotten how long it is), past College Green, down Nassau Street, trying not to collide with any pedestrians. Or cars, trams, vans and bicycles, several of which ring their bells and hoot their horns at us as we dash across the roads. I desperately hope we're on time for Jonty's breakfast.

I'm out of breath by the time we swing around the walls of Trinity College, towards Merrion Square and have to slow down. Jonty gets to the house first, up the granite steps towards the front door. He's about to lift the lion's head knocker when I call up to him from the pavement.

'Jonty! Servants' entrance, remember?' I point at the gate in the railings at street level.

'Forgot about that.' He runs back down the steps, taking them two at a time. I swing open the gate for him and he powers down those steps and raps on the black door with his knuckle.

Seconds later it swings open. Sally stands in the doorway, a huge grin on her face. 'Look at the cut of you both. Bright red faces, how are you.'

'We ran the whole way, Sally,' Jonty says. 'Didn't want to miss my sausages.'

She gives a hearty laugh. 'You're just in time. Quick now. You too, Eliza. Let's get himself the elf all sorted,' she nods at Jonty, 'and then us girls'll have a catch-up over a cuppa. How does that sound?'

'Perfect,' I say.

Sally leads us into the kitchen. There's a plate piled high with sausages and bacon on the large wooden kitchen table and she points at it. 'All yours, Jonty. Tuck in.' He sits and starts eating so fast you'd think he hadn't been fed in days, which he hasn't, not like he was used to.

'Manners, Jonty,' I remind him.

'Sorry, it's so delicious and I'm starving,' he says, his words coming out muffled through his chews.

'Jonty!' I say. 'You know not to talk with your mouth full.'

Sally laughs. 'He's a'right. Have you eaten, pet?' she asks me. 'You look a little pale.'

'I'm fine,' I say, although the smell of Jonty's food is making me feel ravenous.

'Don't fine me,' she says. 'I'll whip you up something tasty once himself is upstairs.' I'm so grateful I almost start crying. I know it's only been a few days, but I've missed Sally's cooking so much. And like Jonty, I'm genuinely hungry.

There's a loud ringing noise and Sally looks at the long panel of bells over the kitchen door. Each one has a number painted under it.

'Seven,' she says. 'The library. Mr Stephens must be ready. Go pop on your uniform, there's a good lad, Jonty. Mr Dalton will be down for you any moment.'

'Will do,' Jonty says. 'Great food, Sally. Any chance of another sausage?'

She frowns, but I can see she's trying not to smile. 'You've already had four. Go on with you.' But she takes one from the frying pan on the Waterford Stanley range and puts in on his plate.

He stuffs the sausage into his mouth and runs out of the

kitchen before Sally can scold him.

'You're going to choke yourself one day, Jonty Kane,' I call after him.

'Thanks for feeding him, Sally,' I say. 'Sorry he's forgotten his manners.'

'My pleasure, pet. Plenty to go around in this place. Mr Pennefeather is a generous man. And I know Jonty's cheeky down here, but Mr Stephens says he's good as gold upstairs. Remember what your poor departed mother used to say: "Street angel, house devil."'

I smile. Mama did say that all right. Jonty has always been good at school. Unless he gets bored of course. But Mama told the teachers to set him harder sums and give him longer books to read, and then he'd settle down.

Mr Dalton walks in. 'Morning, Eliza. Nice to see you again.'

'Morning, Mr Dalton,' I say, a little shyly, remembering what I'd said about Mrs Pennefeather on Friday.

But he just smiles at me. 'Is Jonty ready yet?'

'Ta-da!' Jonty appears in the doorway in a neat black flannel suit, with long trousers and a stiff white collar. He's even wearing a smart black and sky-blue striped tie. I burst out laughing, I can't help it. He looks like a little gentleman and not like my scruffy brother at all. Luckily he sees the funny side too.

'What?' he takes a bow. 'Don't I make a truly fine gentleman?' He purses his lips and strokes an imaginary moustache, twirling the ends.

I start laughing so hard my tummy hurts. 'I'm sorry, Jonty,' I splutter. 'You look very smart. Like Little Lord Fauntleroy.' He's a rich little boy from a book Mama used to read to us.

'I'm glad I amuseth you,' he says, in a ridiculous old-fashioned accent. 'Now I must bid you *adieu*, my studies calleth.'

He gives me an elaborate bow. 'Fair day to you, Lady Eliza.'

My eyes are full of tears from laughing so hard. 'Goodbye, Jonty. Or should I say, My Lord.'

'Jonty?' Mr Dalton walks towards him holding a comb. 'One final thing.'

Jonty rolls his eyes. 'Go on. If you have to.'

Mr Dalton pulls the comb through Jonty's mop of hair with great difficulty, tugging the teeth through the knots, making Jonty wince and yelp.

After he's given Jonty's hair a good going through, Mr Dalton studies the comb's teeth and then clicks his heels together and salutes Jonty. 'Good for battle, Private Kane. Hair combed and nit free.'

'Almost set.' Sally rubs a clean tea towel over Jonty's mouth and straightens his tie with a tug. 'Now you're ready to join the other young gentlemen.'

'Gentlemen?' Jonty grins. 'Have you met Harry and Theo?'

Sally gives a snort. 'Hush, now, Jonty. Best behaviour, mind.'

X X X

Sally's as good as her word and minutes after Jonty has been whooshed upstairs by Mr Dalton I'm tucking into a large plate of bacon and sausages, plus soda bread smothered with butter and a huge mug of milk. It's the best meal I've ever had. I'm practically humming with delight at every mouthful.

'That's it, pet,' she says. 'You eat your fill.' She's rolling out pastry on the table beside me, her hands white from the flour.

'What are you making?' I ask her.

'Pheasant in a pastry plait.' She rolls her eyes. 'Madame's having some fine ladies over for lunch. I cooked the meat filling last night. Hope it's edible, I've never cooked pheasant before. If Madame had her way we'd be eating peasant.'

'Sally!'

'Sorry, my love. But I know you'll keep it to yourself. Let's just say that the lady of the house isn't exactly easy to please. She gets all these fancy recipe ideas from books and wants me to try them out.'

Another bell rings. I look at the panel. This time it's number one.

'Speak of the devil,' Sally says. 'She'll be after fresh tea, no doubt. And another pastry.'

Mr Dalton appears. 'I'll deal with her upstairs,' he tells Sally. 'You catch up with Eliza here.'

Sally puts a delicious-looking pastry with a lemon topping on a plate and Mr Dalton puts it on a silver tray with a pot of tea. He adds a rosebud in a tiny crystal vase.

Holding the tray in front of him, he winks at me. 'Into the lion's den as they say. Until tomorrow, Eliza.'

X X X

'How's your father coping with the move?' Sally asks when I've finished eating. She's now spooning the dark brown meat mix onto a rectangle of raw pastry as long as my arm. It smells rich and sweet.

'I'm worried about him,' I admit. 'His eyesight seems to be getting worse and he won't do anything about it. There's an operation, but he says it's too risky and too expensive. He just sits in his armchair and stares into space most of the day. I'm doing all his work now. I miss college. So much for being an artist and travelling the world.'

Sally straightens her back and wipes her hands on her apron. 'Sometimes life can be hard, pet. Very hard. I know you're tired and fed up. But it won't always be like this. One day the tables will turn and Jonty will be able to support you. Or maybe you'll make a good marriage.'

I stare at her. I love Sally, but I can't get my head around what she's saying. Marriage? Is she mad? I'm far too young to start thinking about that!

'But what about *my* dreams?' I say. 'Don't they mean anything? What if I don't want to get married? Or have Jonty support me? What if I want to be an artist and make my own money?'

Sally sighs. 'It's just the way life is, pet. Sometimes things happen and we have to put our own dreams aside. Best to settle into your new work now, help your father and make the most of things. There are far worse jobs you could be doing, mark my words.'

I feel bad. Sally started working as a maid when she was my age and I know she works really, really hard. Then I think of Annie and all her cleaning and washing jobs and I feel even worse. I've just eaten my fill and this afternoon I get to sit in a quiet workshop on my own and draw for money. I should stop complaining and get on with it!

Maybe Sally's right. Maybe I need to let go of my dreams and accept my new life. But I'm not quite ready – not yet. I put my hand in my pocket and hold my little sketchbook tight for comfort.

X X X

On the way home I spot some of my college classmates on the far side of the road at College Green. I wave at them and shout their names loudly.

'Lilly, Gussie, Amelia, over here!'

They spot me and wave back. They put their heads together and laugh, before disappearing out of sight behind a passing tram.

I wait to cross over to chat to them, but by the time the tram has trundled by they've walked on. I don't have time to run after them so I keep walking towards Sackville Street.

I try not to wonder why they didn't wait or what they were laughing at. Me? Do they know where I live now? Or that I can't afford to go to college any more? Maybe that matters to them. Maybe they don't talk to tenement girls.

No, that's ridiculous, I tell myself. It can't be that, I'm being silly.

But then a thought strikes me. Had I ever met a girl from the tenements before I moved to Henrietta Street? Someone like Annie?

The answer is no.

CHAPTER 10

The largest bee in the world is Megachile pluto.
It is also known as the Flying Bulldog.

That afternoon I find out exactly how hard Annie works. She's leaning against the inside wall of the workshop just after midday, taking a few minutes' rest. Her cheeks are flaming red and pops of sweat dot the side of her face.

'What are you drawing today?' she asks me.

'Take a look if you like,' I say.

'Best not drip all over it.' She laughs and wipes her temples with her apron before leaning over my desk.

I notice her arms are raw red from her hands right up to her elbows from the scorching hot water she's been washing other people's clothes and sheets in – including ours.

Yesterday Papa asked me to find out was there anyone on Henrietta Street who took in washing. I said I'd try to do it myself, but he said it would take too long and I needed to stick to the drawing and painting. Then I thought of Annie.

Although I must admit the thought of her washing all our shirts and drawers still makes me feel a bit funny. But she was delighted with the extra work. And today is wash day.

Earlier she showed me the iron washtub she'd set up over a fire in the yard, the long wooden wash board she rubs the clothes against to get rid of any dirt and the red carbolic soap she uses – it smells like coal tar and made my nose twitch. She has to wash everything, put it through a mangle to get rid of the water and then hang it all up to dry.

Drawing and painting seem easy in comparison.

The Alderman's illumination is coming on well; I just need to add some gold leaf to highlight his name and a few finishing touches.

Today I'm working on a new piece instead as it's far more exciting and, best of all, it's not on pesky vellum! I'm decorating the words of a hymn called 'All Things Bright and Beautiful' with all kinds of flowers and animals. It's for a girl called Margaret-Anne Keyes' sixteenth birthday and I hope she's getting something else too – ribbons, a pretty dress, or at the very least a cake. A decorated hymn isn't much of a gift, if you ask me. But it's paying our bills so I'm glad her parents think it is! I have a few weeks to do it, luckily, so I can take my time.

Annie's eyes scan my work carefully from the top of the large piece of paper to the bottom.

'What's that animal there?' she asks. 'The funny-looking one with the long nose?' She points.

I smile. 'The hymn says "*all* creatures great and small" so I looked up unusual animals in one of Jonty's animal books. That's an anteater. And that's an elephant with a mouse on his back beside the anteater.'

'Aren't elephants afraid of mice? Or so people say.'

'Oh, I think you're right. Just the elephant so. Thanks, Annie.' I take out my piece of putty and rub the mouse off the elephant's back.

Annie studies the drawing for another minute, running her finger carefully over the floral border, with its carefully drawn roses, lilies and daisies. I'm about to ask her to stop in case she smudges my work, but then I remember how clean her hands are from all the washing and scrubbing so I don't.

'It's all so real,' she says. 'I can almost smell the flowers and that bee on the rose looks so lifelike. You're the best artist ever, Eliza. And that's the truth. What's that?' She points at the top of the drawing.

'A dragonfly,' I say. 'I saw one once beside a pond and it was a magical shimmering green. Mama said they're ancient creatures, as old as the dinosaurs.'

'And that animal with the neck? Is it a giraffe? Have you ever seen one in real life, Eliza? I've seen photographs and they look amazing.'

'Yes, in the Zoological Gardens in the Phoenix Park. Have you never been?'

She grins. 'Ha! Where would I be getting the money for the likes of that? But it's on my list. Things I'd like to do one day when I'm rich and famous. As if that'll ever happen. But a girl can dream.'

'What else is on your list?'

'To visit London and see all the fancy ladies in their posh frocks and fancy hats. Even posher than the ladies on Grafton Street, they say. And I'd like to go up in a flying machine one day. Those Wright brothers already have it cracked and I read about a lady from Antrim who flew last year. First lady in the world to make her own flying machine and get it off the ground. Imagine that! When it comes to my dream list, the sky's the limit. Get it?' She hoots with laughter.

I roll my eyes at her bad joke. 'Annie! Anything else on this famous list?'

'Number one is Egypt,' she says. 'I'd like to travel to Egypt, ride on a camel and explore the pyramids. Like Howard Carter. He discovered Hatshepsut's tomb and he reckons there are loads more tombs and mummies and stuff in the Valley of the Kings. In another life I'd study history and be a famous archaeologist like Mr Carter. I love history.'

She looks at me and laughs. 'Eliza! Your face! You look like you've swallowed a goldfish! Tenement girls can have big dreams too, you know. No need to look so surprised.'

'Of course you can,' I say quickly. I can feel my cheeks go red. I *am* surprised, very surprised. I was expecting her dream to be to live in a house with a garden, or to own a farm, or to be rich so she didn't have to clean other people's houses and clothes every day. Not to be an archaeologist.

'I'm a fast reader,' she continues. 'Taught myself pretty much. Hated school, had rotten teachers and besides had to leave at eleven to help at home. I visit the Ladies' Room in the public library whenever I can. There's a nice librarian in there, old fella. He lets me read the history books and the newspapers as long as I'm quiet.'

She looks at me. 'What about your dreams then, Eliza? Must be something to do with art, I'm guessing. Seeing the Mona Lisa in Paris, or the Trevi fountain in Rome or something?'

'I would like to travel all right,' I say. 'And yes, see the Mona Lisa. Although my art tutor says it's really small, not much bigger than your head. But most of all I'd like to finish art college and make my living as an artist. It's not as exciting as being an archaeologist.'

'But your dream could actually come true. That's the difference between us, Eliza. No hope of me being the next Mr Carter, no matter how much I want it. How much do you want to be an artist?'

'What do you mean?'

She looks at me sideways. 'You know exactly what I mean. You have the talent.' She nods down at my drawings. 'Make it happen. Fight for it.'

'It's not as simple as that,' I say a little too sharply.

She shrugs. 'Maybe, maybe not. Anyhows, best get back to work.' She kisses the tips of her fingers and blows them at my drawing. 'Toodles beautiful elephant and dragonfly and giraffe. Back to the wash pot. See you later, Miss Leonardo.' And with a final grin she's gone.

I feel a bit scratchy and huffy. 'Fight for it,' I say out loud. 'Huh! Easy for you to say.' But in my bones I know Annie's right, and that's what's making me so crotchety. Annie and her wonderfully big dreams…

I pull my sketchbook out of my pocket and sit down on my stool. As I start drawing a picture of Annie riding a camel across an Egyptian desert everything else melts away. I'm lost in a world of shading and cross-hatching.

CHAPTER 11

Worker bees start their lives as cleaners, tidying up the honeycomb cells.

Friday, 2 June 1911

'Eliza, you have to come to Dorset Street with me,' Jonty says. 'Right now!'

I look up from the large sheet of vellum I've been trying to draw on. The surface is coarse and bumpy and the lead of my pencil keeps getting stuck and breaking. The elegant swan I'm sketching looks more like a crow. I could do without my brother distracting me. It's Friday afternoon, the end of a long week. Work, cooking, cleaning *and* looking after Jonty and Papa has made me tired and grumpy. I don't know how Annie does it all!

'Don't tell me,' I say with a sigh. 'The McAllisters' cat is stuck up a lamp post again.'

'There are animals all right, but not moggies like Raven.

White stallions and poodles.'

Jonty's eyes are sparkling and I'm starting to get interested. White stallions and poodles?

'What are you doing anyway?' He touches the vellum and immediately pulls his fingers back and rubs them on his tweed breeches. 'Eww! Is that animal skin?'

'Yes, from a calf,' I say. 'It's called vellum.'

He pulls a face. 'Poor calf. Why are you drawing on that?'

'Some businessmen thought it was a good idea. To make their letter look old and special, like the Book of Kells. They liked it so much I have to do another one for a different gentleman. But it's horrible to draw on. I don't know how the ancient monks did it.'

Jonty rolls his eyes. 'Never mind all that boring history stuff. This is urgent!'

There's a loud whooping noise outside, then a burst of clapping and cheering. Jonty jumps around like his feet are on fire.

'Eliza, come on!' he says. 'It's the travelling circus! Remember? From that poster. They're doing a parade and handing out flyers. They must be almost at Rutland Square by now, that's where they're headed. I asked the boy with the big poodle. I wanted it to be a surprise, but if we don't hurry up they'll be gone.'

Jonty's right, we can't miss the circus. It might be our only chance. The vellum will have to wait.

'Come on then, slow coach.' I throw down my pencil and dash out the workshop doors into the yard. Then I get a fit of guilt and spin around in my boots. I run back to the workshop door, quickly bolt it closed, set the padlock and slip the key into the pocket of my skirt where it nestles against my small sketchbook.

'Last one there's a rotten egg,' Jonty calls from the archway to Henrietta Cottages.

'Won't be me!' I sprint to catch up with him, grabbing him by the arm and pulling him backwards so I can overtake him. He may be better at long distances, but I can sprint like the wind.

'Slow coach!' I say as I pass him out.

'Cheat!' he yells. 'No fair. It's only 'cos you're older than me.'

I've always been fast at running, faster than any of the boys. I used to win races in Rathmines National School all the time before the master stopped the girls taking part.

I come to an abrupt stop as soon as I reach Dorset Street.

Two of the most beautiful horses I've ever seen are walking towards us, their coats and flowing manes snow-white, their heads topped with fluffy white ostrich feathers. Their white leather bridles and saddles are studded with silver stars. They are lifting their legs in time with the jaunty music coming from the circus organ, on a special wagon behind them.

The two people riding the stallions are just as regal, like a circus king and queen. There's a stocky dark-haired man in a top hat and tails, with a scarlet waistcoat and matching kerchief poking out of his pocket.

'He must be the ringmaster,' I tell Jonty. I remember his name from the poster. 'Mr Zozimus Wilde.'

And on the horse beside the ringmaster is the most extraordinary-looking woman, like a character from a pre-Raphaelite painting. A shock of thick red hair frames her heart-shaped face. There's a peacock-blue felt hat perched on her head with acres of matching-coloured jewelled netting running down her black velvet jacket and flowing across the horse's back. She looks like a fairy queen.

Jonty comes to a standstill by my side. He gives a deep sigh of pleasure as he watches the horses and their riders stride by us. He starts humming and singing along with the circus organ, making up his own lyrics. 'Dee-dee diddely dee-dee, dee-dee. Circus music, dogs and horses, clowns and lions, diddely diddely dee!'

'Lions?' I look behind the circus organ, but I can only see a clown and some jugglers. 'Where?'

'Here!' A boy in a suit and straw boater presses a circus leaflet into my hand and jabs at the drawing of a lion with his finger.

He's short, not much taller than Jonty, but from his swagger and confidence he's definitely older. There's a trail of dogs of all shapes and sizes yapping happily at his white leather dancing shoes.

'The most ferocious lions in the whole entire universe,' he adds. 'Even London town, that's my neck of the woods.' He sounds like he's from London all right, there's even a swagger to his accent.

He gives me an enormous grin. 'Will you come? To the greatest show on earth?'

He has bright cornflower-blue eyes and his smile is so friendly and open I can't help but smile right back. 'Maybe,' I say.

'Magic!' he says, giving me a wink.

I try not to blush. A London boy just winked at me. I can't wait to tell Annie!

'Do you have any elephants?' Jonty asks him.

'Nah, Jessie's not with us any more,' the boy says. 'Gone to the elephant graveyard in the sky. But we've the best performing dogs this side of the Atlantic Ocean. Want to see some tricks?'

He turns towards the large black poodle and says, 'Dance with me, Pepper, there's a girl? Hup, hup! That's it, magic!'

The dog springs onto her back paws and gives the boy her front paws. The boy starts to waltz along to the circus organ, with the dog following his steps.

'Splendid day for a dance, Pepper,' the boy says to the dog, in a posh accent. 'I do love a good waltz.'

Jonty and I laugh.

'I see you've met our troublemaker, Albert.' The clown walking just behind the boy raises a huge red clown shoe and gives the boy an exaggerated kick on the bottom.

'Eh, eh, Coco!' the boy protests.

'Move along, Albert! Let your new friends meet the wonder that is Coco. Which would be little old me.'

I look closer and realise it's a woman under all the white

clown make-up. She pats her chest, spreading her hands like starfish and giving a cheesy grin. She points at the large fabric rose attached to the lapel of her baggy black and white chequered jacket and asks Jonty, 'Care to smell my flower?'

'Yes!' Jonty grins, leans forwards and is treated to a squirt of water in the face.

'Hey!' Jonty cries, wiping the drips out of his eyes. He grins. 'Great trick.'

We follow the circus parade to Rutland Square and down Sackville Street. Every now and then Albert walks beside us, dancing with Pepper and then balancing his smallest dog on his head.

'Is Pepper a poodle?' Jonty asks Albert as we pass the General Post Office.

'That's right,' Albert says. 'A standard poodle. And this fine lady on my head is Miss Primrose, a Jack Russell. Princess Ellie here is a Russian Wolfhound.' He nods at the largest dog, a silvery grey animal the size of a miniature pony. 'And Salty with the sailor hat, he's a boxer. And as Coco said, I'm Albert, their trainer otherwise known as their dogs' body.'

He gives a click with his tongue and another wink.

'Do they like doing tricks?' I ask.

'Try stopping 'em,' he says. He takes Miss Primrose off his head and places her gently on the ground, then says, 'Hup, hup, everyone,' and raises both arms in the air. The dogs all jump onto their hind legs and start dancing. 'Magic!' he tells his dogs.

I give a delighted laugh. 'How clever.'

'Magic!' Jonty says.

I've never heard him say that before. I smile to myself.

Mama always said Jonty is like a magpie with words, picks them up all over the place. He's picked up Albert's word.

Albert digs into his pocket and pulls out a waxed paper bag. He throws each of them a tiny piece of pale meat from the bag. It looks like chicken. I try not to stare at it too hard. It makes me hungry just looking at it. We haven't had chicken for weeks.

I'm glad of the distraction when Albert says 'Hup, hup,' again.

All the dogs apart from Pepper jump onto their front paws and balance for a few seconds before dropping their back paws to the ground. Albert rewards them all with a treat, even Pepper.

'She's got a crook front paw, don't you, girl? Can't do that one any more, can you?' He rubs her behind her ears and she looks up at him adoringly.

'That's incredible,' Jonty says. 'How do you train them to do that?'

Albert grins. 'Patience. And a lotta, lotta chicken.'

We reach O'Connell Bridge and follow the parade as it crosses the River Liffey and turns right, along the quays. As we cross, a barge full of barrels slowly chugs under the arches of the bridge, men sitting on their cargo, smoking pipes and eating. It's a still day and I can smell their tobacco in the air.

'We'd better go back now,' I tell Jonty. 'Papa will start to wonder where we are.'

'Just a few more minutes, please?' Jonty puts his hands together and pleads with me.

'Fine. But I've no coins for the Ha'penny Bridge so don't ask.'

As we walk along the quays Pepper starts barking frantically at the barge and races towards the wall at Wood Quay.

'Pepper, come back!' Albert shouts.

But it's no use, Pepper has scaled the wall and there's an almighty splash.

'Pepper!' Albert sprints towards the wall and Jonty and I dash after him. Pepper is in the river, floundering to keep her head above water.

'It's her paw. She's finding it hard to swim.' He swears under his breath, staring at the water. 'I can't swim or I'd go in after her. She'll be all right, Albert, strong dog like that,' he tells himself.

But the water is choppy from the barge's wake and she's clearly struggling.

Coco appears beside us. 'What's happening?' she asks.

'Pepper's in the water,' Albert says. 'She must have smelt something to eat on one of the barges. Nose like a bloodhound that one.'

'A boat will pick her up,' Coco says. 'There'll be one passing in no time, you'll see.'

We wait a few seconds, but nothing. No chugging, no boats. And Pepper seems to be tiring, her doggie paddle only just about keeping her afloat. And then she starts yelping in pain and barking wildly.

'She's calling for help,' Albert says. He starts to pull off his jacket. 'Maybe I could give this swimming lark a go. How hard can it be?'

But before he finishes taking his arm out of the sleeve there's a second splash. I look down. It's Jonty! He's in the water, swimming towards Pepper.

'Jonty!' I scream. 'Be careful. If a boat hits you, you're done for.'

But he ignores me and keeps on swimming. He has a strong stroke; Mama loved swimming and taught us both in the sea baths at Blackrock.

He's almost reached Pepper who has been swept into the

middle of the river by the current when there's the chug-chug of a barge.

I start shouting with all my might. 'There's a boy in the water! Boy in the water!' But the men on the barge don't show any signs of hearing me.

'Albert, can you make the dogs bark?' I ask him.

He nods, understanding immediately. He drops to his knees, throws his head back and starts to howl like a wolf.

The dogs sing out an ear-splitting chorus of howling and barking. The men on the barge look over and I point frantically at Jonty in the water. One of the men shouts an order to the captain and the barge immediately swerves to the right and then slows down. Another man throws Jonty a rope.

I can't hear what the man's saying over the noise of the boat's engine, but his face looks friendly. He's pointing at Pepper and shaking his head.

'Looks like he's telling your brother he's mad to jump in after a dog,' Albert says.

'I think you're right.' I realise I've been practically holding my breath, terrified at the thought of the boat hitting Jonty. I take a few big gulps of air. I suddenly realise I couldn't bear life without my brother. My eyes fill with tears of relief and

I blink them away.

'You all right, Miss?' Albert asks.

'Eliza,' I say. 'Eliza Kane. And yes, I'm quite all right, thank you. I just got a fright. And well done to your clever dogs. Quite the howl you have too!'

Albert gives an elaborate bow. 'Why thank you.'

'What's all the commotion?' It's the fairy queen, followed by the ringmaster, still on their white horses.

'This is 'Liza,' Albert tells them. Her brother only went and saved Pepper from drowning. Jumped in after her, didn't he?' He points down at the granite steps, where a docker is helping Jonty out of the water. Jonty has his arms hugged firmly round Pepper's waist and isn't letting go.

They dismount, hand their horses' reins to Coco and join us by the quay wall.

As soon as Jonty and Pepper are both on dry land I call down, 'Well done, Jonty!' as the docker helps him up the steps and then jumps back onto his boat.

He grins up at me. 'Water's lovely. You should try it.'

Pepper jumps up and gives Jonty's cheek an almighty lick and we all laugh.

'Bravo!' the fairy queen says. 'Your brother is quite the hero.'

Her voice is surprisingly low and warm and she speaks with an accent, Italian I think. 'She smiles. 'And heroes must be rewarded. Ringside seats for both of you. The circus awaits.'

CHAPTER 12

After being cleaners, worker bees are promoted to feeding the bee
larvae that have hatched out of eggs with pollen and honey.

'Hurry up, Eliza,' Jonty says. 'I can see the Big Top.'

Jonty's right, the circus tent is peeping out from between
the houses on Granby Row and the Black Church. It's
pitched on the fields behind the church and the sight of the
jaunty red and white stripes is making my fingers tingle with
excitement.

There's a crowd of people heading towards the entrance,
lots of families with children, the little ones clinging to their
mothers' hands tightly. Eager faces all shining, but none as
bright as Jonty's.

Music is playing on the steam organ, Jonty's favourite
circus song. He's been humming it constantly over the last
few days – *dee-dee, diddely dee-dee, dee-dee.*

We were so excited last night we could barely sleep. And

now we're here!

Papa was a bit suspicious when Jonty arrived back squelching after his river rescue. I knew he wouldn't approve of us following the circus down the quays or of Jonty risking his life to save a dog, so we kept it to ourselves. Jonty told Papa he'd jumped into a puddle, but it had turned out to be deeper than he'd thought. It's exactly the kind of daft thing Jonty would do so Papa believed him!

The line moves quickly and within minutes we're handing our tickets to the man at the door. He's wearing black trousers tucked into black knee-high boots, a white shirt with a red kerchief tied at his neck and a matching red waistcoat.

The man looks at the tickets and smiles at us. 'Complimentary ringside tickets, best in the 'ouse.' From his accent he sounds Italian too, like the fairy queen. 'You must know someone very special,' he adds.

'Albert,' I say. 'Jonty here saved his dog, Pepper.'

The man grins. 'Ah the famous Jonty. I hear all about you. I am Luca, friend of Albert. He say if you like to visit the animals after the show he give you special tour. Yes?'

'Yes!' we both say together and then laugh as Luca puts his hands over his ears, grinning. It was a rather loud yes!

As we walk inside the tent there's a strong smell of paraffin lamps and horses. There are rows and rows of wooden benches around a central ring, filled with yellow sawdust.

'There's Albert,' Jonty says. I look over to the right where he's pointing. Albert is helping people find their seats. We make our way towards him.

As soon as Albert spots us he gives a huge grin. "Liza, Jonty, you made it! Magic! Follow me.'

He shows us to a wooden bench inches away from the wooden circus ring. 'Have to dash but you'll see me soon,' he says. 'I'll be the one running after the circus mutts, trying to keep 'em under control. And I'll see if I can sneak out to you before that too.'

Once he's gone, we sit on the bench and Jonty swings his legs, his boots catching the sawdust underfoot, spraying it up into the air.

'I wonder who will be on first,' he says. 'I was up all last night thinking about it. My money's on Mr Wilde because it's his circus.'

I smile at him. 'Let's see if you're right.'

The tent fills up quickly. The expectant hum of the crowd gets louder and louder. A family sits down on the bench beside us, a well-dressed gentleman and lady with a little girl in a frothy white lace party dress with a straw hat topping her dark curls.

'Will there be horses?' says the little girl. She's sitting directly beside Jonty.

'I think so,' says her mother. 'You like horses, don't you?'

'I want to marry a horse,' the girl says, making her mother laugh.

'There are lots of horses,' Jonty tells the girl confidently. 'They do all kinds of tricks too.'

'Have you been to this circus before?' the girl asks him.

'Albert from the circus is our friend,' he says. 'He trains the performing dogs.'

'Gosh!' The girl gazes at Jonty adoringly. 'Lucky you. I'm Alice May. What's your name?'

'Jonty. Pleased to meet you, Alice May.'

The father gives Jonty a different kind of look, not a nice one. He leans across the girl's mother and whispers something to the girl who then goes silent and stares down at her feet. Luckily Jonty's eyes are fixed on the red velvet curtains where the performers will enter the ring, so he doesn't notice.

We don't have long to wait. Minutes later we hear the

familiar jaunty tune, *dee-dee, diddely, dee-dee, dee-dee*. When the song finishes there's a clash of the cymbals and Mr Wilde runs through the red curtain in a shiny black dinner jacket with tails and a top hat. He cracks his whip on the sawdust.

'I was right, it's Mr Wilde first,' Jonty says, jumping to his feet and clapping furiously.

'Ladies and gentlemen,' Mr Wilde booms. 'I am Mr Zozimus Wilde. Welcome to our famous travelling circus. Today you will meet true wonders of the world, a menagerie of animals from all over the globe. Ferocious lions, a snake from the South American rainforest, and the greatest human talent that has even been seen. Let the show begin! First, Madam Ada and our Arabian stallions.'

Alice May squeals beside us. 'Horses!'

The curtain parts and six white horses gallop into the ring. Riding on the back of one of first animals is a woman in a green velvet dress. Her flaming red hair streams out behind her. Madam Ada!

'It's the woman from the quays who gave us the tickets,' Jonty says.

'That's right,' I say. 'Doesn't she look magnificent?'

Mr Wilde throws his whip to Luca and as the stallions

gallop along beside him, he runs with them for a moment before pulling himself onto the back of the horse beside Madam Ada.

Seconds later Mr Wilde and Madam Ada are both standing on their horses' backs. The horses canter around and around the ring, only inches away from us, their hooves thundering against the sawdust, Mr Wilde and Madam Ada still on their feet. It's quite the sight!

After a few more laps Mr Wilde and Madam Ada sit back down on the horses, wave to the crowd and disappear back through the curtain. Jonty sighs happily.

As we wait for the next act, someone sits down beside me. It's Albert.

He leans in towards us. 'What'cha make of it so far?'

'Magic,' Jonty says. 'Best thing I've ever seen.' My brother's grinning from cheek to cheek and his eyes are shining like diamonds.

Albert smiles. 'And it's only getting started. Wait till you see Lulu's act. She's on next. She'll be wearing a sparkly leotard.'

'What's a leotard?' I ask.

He smiles. 'You'll see.'

CHAPTER 13

Finally worker bees become foragers, collecting water, pollen and nectar for the hive. They do this for the rest of their short lives, around five weeks.

Mr Wilde strides through the curtains and into the ring once more. 'Prepare to be amazed. I now present our African Princess, Miss Lulu the Human Butterfly. She will perform her famous iron-jaw act for your delight.'

Lulu runs through the curtain and we all clap and cheer. The paraffin lamps pick out the glittering golden fringing on her golden costume. So that's a leotard.

'Is Miss Lulu really from Africa?' Jonty asks Albert.

'Nah, Bristol. But her grandfather was. Taken as a slave a long time ago.'

Jonty's eyes open wider. 'Gosh, poor man.'

The band starts playing a gentle piece of music, a waltz this time. A rope appears above Lulu's head. It's being lowered by Luca. On the end of the rope is what looks like a leather strap about the length of my hand. Lulu takes the strap and puts it into her mouth. Then Luca pulls on the rope and slowly hoists her into the air, her whole body hanging by her teeth.

'Ouch!' Jonty says. 'That must hurt.'

'They don't call it iron jaw for nothin',' Albert says.

Luca lifts her higher and higher, almost to the top of the circus tent. Then she starts whirling like a spinning top, faster and faster, the sequins on her leotard catching the light from the paraffin lamps and making sparkles dance around the tent. For a second it reminds me of the crystal chandelier in the Pennefeathers' hall.

Luca then lowers her down and Lulu removes the strap from her mouth and takes a bow. The tent erupts with clapping and cheering.

'My cue to skidoo,' Albert says. 'Did Luca tell you to come behind the curtain after the show to see the animals?'

'Yes,' I say.

'Magic.' He gives us both a wink. 'Watch out for us in the ring. I'll give you a wave.'

Lulu takes her final bow and finds Coco standing beside her pointing up at the trapeze and her own mouth, which has a ring of red clown paint around it.

'You want to try hanging from your teeth, Coco?' Lulu asks her.

Coco nods furiously. Luca lowers the strap and it hits Coco on the head. She falls onto the ground and everyone laughs. Coco then chases the strap around the ring, as it continues to run away from her and hit her on the head.

'Too bad, Coco,' Lulu says. 'I don't think you're cut out for iron jaw.'

Coco puts on her best sad face and waves goodbye to Lulu who disappears through the curtains. She pretends to think, putting her finger on her head, then takes a chair from the side of the stage and stands on it.

When the seat falls in, she lands in the middle of the chair's frame, then jumps back up and lands on the front edge of the frame.

'Incredible!' Jonty says. 'Did you see that?'

Pepper runs through the red curtain and bites Coco on the bottom. Coco's face twists into a curl of agony and outrage! Jonty is laughing so much his eyes are watering. Even the crosspatch man beside us can't help but laugh.

'Isn't Coco magic?' Jonty asks me.

'Magic,' I agree. 'What an actress.'

Mr Wilde strides back into the ring. 'Off you go, Coco, that's right. Try not to trip. Oops, up you get.' Coco stumbles and tumbles right through the red curtains, Pepper running after her, snapping at her bottom.

We watch Luca and Franco juggling and Coco doing more funny tricks before Mr Wilde comes back on.

'See you after the interval for our brave Lion Queen,' he says. 'All the way from Russia, it's Miss Karina Zemkova.'

x x x

During the interval, a circular metal cage is constructed just inside the ring. Some of the circus troupe including Luca and Franco are selling sweets in little paper bags. I know this because the zingy sweet smell of my favourites, sherbet lemons, is wafting towards me from the bag in Alice May's hands. My mouth waters.

One day, I promise myself. One day I'll have enough money to buy sherbet lemons whenever I want to.

Luca passes by us and winks at me. Next thing I feel something land in my lap and I look down. It's a bag of sweets! Inside are at least ten sherbet lemons. He's gone before I get the chance to thank him.

'Here.' I pass Jonty one carefully and he places it in his

palm looks down at it in awe, like it's a precious gem.

'We haven't had sweets since Mama, well, you know...' He breaks off for a second, then says 'Can we keep some for George and Sid?'

Jonty has such a good heart. He's already best friends with Annie's brothers, playing with them every day on the street after school.

'Course you can,' I say. 'And I'll keep some for Annie. How about we just have two each? One now and one after the show to celebrate. And save the rest.'

'Sounds good to me.' Jonty closes his eyes and drops the sweet onto his pink tongue. 'Delicious,' he says, moving the sweet around in his mouth.

I pop mine in my own mouth and suck hard, the zing of the lemon making my taste buds dance. We sit in silence, happily sucking our sweets.

X X X

'Ladies and gentlemen, girls and boys, this is an important announcement,' Mr Wilde says, after re-entering the ring. 'African lions are very, very dangerous. One false move and our Lion Queen could be crushed by their ferocious jaws. I need you to remain quiet, please! Any sudden noise could be fatal.' The whole tent goes deathly silent.

'Now,' he says, 'I invite Miss Karina to bring on her fearsome lions.'

Miss Karina climbs through a small gate in the cage and closes it firmly behind her.

'Is that a real leopard skin over her leotard?' Jonty asks me. It's held in place by a thick black belt.

'I think so,' I say.

He doesn't look very impressed.

There is a caged tunnel leading from behind the red curtains. Miss Karina gives a crack of her whip and four lions pad down the tunnel, towards the central cage.

She gives another crack and they pace around the cage in a line, the largest one, with a shaggy mane first, the other three female lions – lionesses – following behind him.

'They don't look all that fearsome,' Jonty says, his eyes locked on the four big cats. 'They seem a bit sleepy. More like pussy cats.'

I give a laugh. 'Jonty!'

'I think they've just been fed. But if they can't be in the wild at least they're happy being circus lions.'

'How can you tell?'

He shrugs. 'I just can.'

I believe him. My brother has always had a special way with animals. That's why losing Oboe upset him so much, Oboe was his best friend.

One day Oboe came in from the garden limping. Jonty studied him for a moment and then lifted his front right paw and pulled a large thorn out of the black fleshy pad. Oboe licked Jonty's face, clearly delighted.

When the white bit around one of Oboe's eyes went red, Jonty soaked it using Papa's eye drops. It worked!

Miss Karina clearly has a way with animals too. When she cracks her whip again, the lions leap onto large metal stools and give an almighty roar.

'This is Rex.' Miss Karina points her whip at the male lion. 'King of the jungle. I will now put my head into the mouth of Rex, yes? This is highly dangerous so I must prepare.' She closes her eyes and puts her hands together, like she's praying.

Jonty is smiling to himself.

'What?' I ask him.

'Look at the way Rex is gazing at her. He's not going to bite off her head. I bet she's the one who feeds him and looks after him.'

Jonty is right. Miss Karina makes a big performance about putting her head in Rex's mouth, but he simply lets her.

'I bet she gives him a big bone to chew on after each show,' Jonty says. 'That's what I'd do if I was a lion tamer.'

Next up is Albert and his performing dogs. He makes sure to catch our eyes and wink at us several times as he and Pepper and the pack make everyone laugh and gasp, especially when Miss Primrose runs around an open parasol, which Albert holds over his head.

'And now,' Mr Wilde says when Albert and his dogs have left the ring. 'A lady who with her voice and her beauty can coax the very bees from their hives. I present to you my remarkable wife, Madam Ada, our very own bee charmer.

'I assure you, once the bees are on Madam Ada's person, all are safe. But if they swarm in your direction, their combined stings could be deadly. So please stay very quiet and very still.'

The tent immediately hushes and Madam Ada rides through the curtains on the back of one of the white stallions. There's a large dark patch around her neck, standing out against her pale skin. She circles the ring, ever so slowly, stopping her horse every few steps and facing the audience.

As she comes closer to where we are sitting I realise the dark patch is made up of bees – thousands of them – all clustered closely together around her neck and sweeping down over her chest like a strange buzzing beard. As she moves towards us the tiny animals' hum gets louder and louder.

Madam Ada positions her horse directly in front of us. For a second the whole world goes quiet and all I can hear is the hum of the bees. As I watch, a curl of them break away from Madam Ada in a swirling line like a wisp of smoke and fly in my direction.

They hover in front of me, swooping and spiralling in the air. It's almost like they're dancing for me. But it must be my imagination. Bees don't dance! And it's certainly my imagination when I hear, 'Welcome, little one' in my head.

I lock eyes with Madam Ada for a moment and she smiles at me, her eyes wise and kind. I blink. And then the spell is broken and the bees fly back to their swarm. It's like I've just woken up from a strange dream.

Madam Ada is still there, smiling. I smile back. Jonty is too mesmerised by the bees on Madam Ada's neck to notice so I nudge him.

'Madam Ada's smiling at you,' I tell him.

'Gosh, right.' He tears his eyes away from the bees and grins at her. She gives him a little nod, which must be no joke with a scarf of bees around your neck!

As she moves away from us Jonty asks me, 'How does she keep the bees attached to her like that? I reckon there's sugar water or honey on her skin. I'm going to ask her later.'

'She might not want to tell you her secret,' I warn him.

Jonty shrugs. 'If you don't ask, you don't get.'

It's what Mama used to say when Papa asked her why she insisted on calling on all the neighbours, looking for clothes, shoes and food to help the poorer families in Dublin city.

'We were put onto this earth to be kind and to help each other, Thomas,' Mama would say. 'And kind we shall be.'

With a start I realise Mama could have been collecting for families on Henrietta Street. Like Annie and her brothers. Maybe even like us.

Madam Ada's horse walks backwards out of the ring, through the red curtains and she disappears. Jonty jumps to his feet, clapping and cheering wildly. Within seconds, the whole tent erupts into a standing ovation, the whoops are deafening.

The man beside us sniffs and stays seated. 'They're only bees.'

But his wife is practically jumping up and down with delight. 'I've never seen anything like it,' she says, 'such mastery of those insects. Magical.'

'Do you believe in magic, Mummie?' Alice May asks. 'Daddy says it's all piffle.'

'I certainly do, my darling,' she says. 'What's life without a bit of magic, eh?' She gives her daughter a hug.

X X X

There's more: acrobatics, giant snakes and the Flying Fanzinis on trapeze – it's spectacular and breathtaking and I never want it to end, but sadly it must.

For the finale, the whole circus troupe come on (minus the lions) and perform one last time, to say goodbye. After they finish, there's another rousing standing ovation. And then the spell is broken and the tent starts to clear as the crowd heads back to real life outside the big top. But not us: we stay in our seats. We get to hold on to the circus magic for a little bit longer.

'Are you not going home?' Alice May asks Jonty.

'No, we're waiting to see our circus friends,' he says proudly.

'You're the luckiest duckers in the whole wide world,' she says.

When Alice May and her parents have gone Jonty says 'We *are* lucky, aren't we?'

'Very lucky,' I tell him. I think about everything that's happened to my brother in the last few months – Mama dying, losing Oboe, having to leave Rathmines and go to school at the Pennefeathers' house – he's gone through a lot. He deserves all the luck in the world.

Albert appears beside us again. 'Ready to go behind the curtains?' he says.

'Too right!' says Jonty.

CHAPTER 14

The queen bee's job is to produce more bees for the colony and she may lay up to a million eggs in her lifetime.

As we follow Albert through the curtains I'm so excited I'm practically holding my breath. But it's not at all what I expected! We're in a smaller, rectangular tent that smells of paraffin oil and animals. There are bits and bobs from the different circus acts stacked in piles, like open wooden travelling trunks full of juggling clubs and the little stools and jumps for Albert's performing dogs. It's like a circus hardware shop in here!

Some of the circus artists are also in the tent. Coco is sitting on an upended metal bucket, carefully taking off Pepper's fancy lace collar. She spots us and gives a friendly wave.

I'm a bit disappointed to be honest – it's all so practical and ordinary. I guess I was expecting a little more magic. But Jonty's eyes are wide with wonder, taking in every little detail.

'I'll show you some of the animals,' Albert says and we

follow him outside. The animal wagons are parked in a semi-circle around the muddy central open space. Behind, I can see the white horses grazing in a roped off area of the green.

'What would you like to see first?' Albert asks. 'The big cats I'm guessing.'

'Yes, please!' I say.

He smiles. 'Beast wagons it is.' He leads up towards a large wooden animal wagon painted wine red. It has thick iron bars running along one side. Inside the wagon Karina's three lionesses are lying on the straw, yawning or dozing.

'Meet Eloise, Rosie and Lucille,' Albert says, pointing at each lioness. 'Hello, girls. Wakey, wakey.'

They lift their heads and look at him, mildly interested before nestling back down in their straw.

'They get tired after shows,' Albert says. 'Don't blame them. It is pretty tiring, entertaining all you lot.' He smiles at me and Jonty.

Jonty presses his face against the bars to get a better look.

'Careful, Jonty,' I say. 'They may look like pussy cats, but they're still wild animals and they don't know you.'

'No idea of their own strength neither,' Albert says, 'or that humans are lighter and more breakable. They're devoted to Karina and she's had her fill of nasty scratches and knocks, but nothing too serious. Lucille nearly tore her last trainer's cheek off one day with her claws. She was only playing, but it was a nasty injury, took dozens of stitches to fix the poor woman's face back together. Left some nasty scars. And frightened her half to death. She had to leave the circus because of it.'

I wince. 'Poor lady. Karina must be brave.'

'Very brave,' he says. 'You have to be to work with the big cats. Rex wouldn't put a finger on her though.'

He shows us to the next wagon where Rex is stretched out on the straw, resting. He perks up when he sees us and rubs his mane against the bars, making thick golden strands poke through.

'Can I touch his mane?' Jonty asks.

Albert looks around. 'Go on, but quick. And keep your hand outside the bars, you hear me. If Karina spots us, she'll throw a canary.'

Jonty strokes Rex's mane, his full being concentrated on the animal's eyes. 'There boy,' he's saying in a gentle, soothing voice. 'Do you dream of the African plains? I bet you do.

Lying in the hot sun with your pride. You're such a beautiful animal.' Jonty reaches in and rubs Rex behind his ear, like he used to do with Oboe.

Jonty! My whole body goes rigid. I want to shout at him to stop, but I don't want to scare Rex and make him scratch Jonty or even worse. I look over at Albert whose mouth is stretched out, tense.

'Arm out now, Jonty,' Albert says in a low, even voice. 'Slow and calm, that's it, good lad.'

Once Jonty's arm is safely beside his body Albert grabs my brother's shoulders and shakes him so hard Jonty's teeth almost rattle in his skull.

'Ain't you been listening to a word? That's a wild animal, Jonty. Not to be trifled with. He don't know your smell yet and he's half blind. For all he knows your arm was a bone with fresh meat on it for him to chew on. From now on keep your hands to yourself, got it?'

'Sorry,' Jonty mumbles, face bright red. He looks like he's about to cry.

'He didn't mean any harm,' I say quickly. 'And he'll never do it again, will you, Jonty?'

Jonty shakes his head. My brother's blinking quickly and

pressing his lips together hard, fighting to hold back his tears.

Albert softens. 'The circus can be a dangerous place. You have to follow the rules. Got it? My fault too. Should never have said you could stroke his mane. And I'm sorry for shaking you, Jonty. We good?'

Jonty nods silently, but he's still staring down at his feet.

'Look at me, Jonty,' Albert says. 'No harm done. It's forgotten.' He bops Jonty gently on the arm. 'You need to learn to bounce back quickly to work in the circus. We speak our mind. No time for grudges or sulking.' He nudges Jonty with his shoulder and Jonty manages a small smile.

'Follow me,' Albert says, 'horses next. Less likely to bite your arm off.'

The horses are roaming free in the roped-off field behind the wagons. Without their fancy bridles and saddles they look less formal, but their size and the elegant way they hold their heads and necks makes them look powerful and magical. They're certainly unlike any horses I've seen before.

'Arabian stallions,' Albert says as we watch them pulling mouthfuls of hay out of the bales and chewing the strands with their strong teeth that look like ivory piano keys.

'Beautiful,' Jonty whispers. He's gazing at the horses in awe.

'Trained from foals,' Albert adds. 'Best in the world. Zozimus' grandfather was an officer in the cavalry. Zozimus is a natural with horses, loves 'em to bits. Aunt Ada too. Although not as much as her bees.'

'Is she really your aunt?' I ask him.

'Nah, but as good as. Circus family.'

'And where does she keep the bees?' I look around the edges of the field, but I don't see any telltale hives.

Albert grins. 'Come and see. But don't get too close and keep your hands to yourself this time.'

x x x

To the right of the green, behind what Albert calls the beast wagons, Madam Ada is standing with her back to us, facing a large white linen sheet. It's spread at her feet like a ghostly picnic rug. A man is standing beside her. He's wearing a hat with white netting surrounding it and thick white gloves that cover his hands and wrists. Even with all that gear on, from the stiffness of his body he looks pretty nervous.

He's a giant too, his head almost reaching the top of the dark red wagon beside him, which is covered with a curve of faded green tarpaulin, like a Romany caravan. The only person I've ever seen that height is Annie's friend, Tall Joe. I squint and try to make out the man's face through the mesh. I think it *is* Tall Joe!

'Is that…' I start to ask Albert, but he shushes me.

'Quiet now,' he says, his eyes fixed on Madam Ada. 'She's de-bearding.'

As we watch Madam Ada whips her upper body towards the sheet. Bees drop off her shoulders in buzzing clumps.

'That is seriously weird,' Jonty murmurs.

Madam Ada does this three times until most of the bees are crawling around on the sheet. Tall Joe brushes the last remaining bees off her with a soft brush and then stands well back.

Madam Ada reaches her hands to the back of her neck and unties the leather necklace strap. Suspended from it is a tiny cage. She holds it in her hand while Tall Joe lowers the wooden flap at the back of the wagon and swings himself up.

Inside are three small wooden houses. I've seen them before with Mama – beehives. He lifts the lid off one of the hives, reaches inside and takes out one of the frames. There's honeycomb suspended inside it and the sweet, warm smell drifts towards us.

'Can you smell the honey, Jonty?' I whisper.

He nods without taking his eyes off Madam Ada, mesmerised by what's happening in front of him.

Madam Ada opens the catch on the tiny cage, pinches her fingers together and takes out a bee. It's larger than the other bees, almost twice the size.

'A bee? Amazing!' I say in my head, but as Albert is shushing me it must have been out loud. 'Sorry,' I murmur.

He smiles. 'S'all right,' he whispers. 'First time I saw it I was shocked too. It's the Queen. Each hive has its own Queen. The workers from the hive always follow their own Queen. They smell her. Bees' smell is top notch. A hundred times better than ours, according to Aunt Ada.'

'Like dogs,' Jonty says.

'That's right, Jonty,' Albert says. 'Just like dogs.'

'*Ciao*, Queen Augusta,' Madam Ada says as she carefully places the bee into the frame and then nods at Tall Joe who slots the frame back into the hive.

'Does each Queen have a name?' I ask Albert.

He nods. 'And Aunt Ada seems to be able to tell each of them apart. I have no idea how. When it comes to bees, she's got some sort of spooky magic.'

'Now what?' I ask.

'Wait and see.'

Tall Joe pulls the sheet heavy with bees carefully towards the hive. They start to buzz, louder and louder and within seconds hundreds of them take off and fly into the hive, so close together their humming bodies look like one mysterious black animal.

'Home again, home again, jiggedy-jig,' Albert says. 'They'd follow their Queen anywhere. Even into a circus ring.'

'So that's the secret,' Jonty murmurs.

As the bees fly home to their hive, Tall Joe takes off his net hat and shoves it under his arm. He and Madam Ada walk over to join us.

'*Ciao*,' Madam Ada says, her green eyes twinkling. 'Dog hero and sister, *tesori*, my treasures.' She waves her right hand and drops into a theatrical bow, making us laugh. She straightens up again.

'Otherwise known as Jonty and 'Liza,' Albert tells Tall Joe.

Tall Joe grins. 'Oh I know Eliza all right. Friend of my Annie's and I've seen the lad with George and Sid. They're tenement, like me.'

I can't wait to tell Annie what he just said – friend of *my* Annie's. From the way his eyes lit up when he mentioned her name, he's definitely sweet on her.

'Hello again, Tall Joe,' I say. 'And thank you for allowing us watch you rehouse your bees, Madam Ada. It's one of the most marvellous things I've ever seen. We won't tell anyone how you create your bee beard. Your secret's safe with us, isn't it, Jonty?'

Jonty purses his lips and pretends to turn a key in his mouth 'lock', just like he saw Albert do in the circus tent, making us all laugh.

Madam Ada smiles. 'My pleasure. My honeybees never cease to amaze me too, remarkable creatures.' There are still a few bees hovering around her head and one is sitting on her shoulder but she doesn't seem to notice.

'Do they ever sting you when they're crawling on your skin?' Jonty asks.

'Sometimes,' she admits. 'But bees don't sting all that often – they die when they lose their sting. Part of their bodies gets left behind with the stinger – a tragedy. Poor Joseph comes a cropper quite often though. Not your favourite job, is it, *Tesoro*, working with my honeys?'

Tall Joe just grins. 'I'm at your service, Madam Ada. Your wish is my command.'

She's smiling at him so fondly it makes my heart squeeze. I wish someone would look at me like that.

A dark shadow passes in front of my eyes and the next thing I know something has landed on my nose. I stare at it cross-eyed, which makes me feel a bit dizzy. It's one of Madam Ada's honeybees so I don't want to be rude and swat it off like I normally would.

Instead I stay very still. I can feel the honeybee's tiny feet tickling the skin of my nose as it walks down it and I stiffen. I now see how Tall Joe feels, working with Madam Ada's honeybees. In awe but also terrified of being stung.

I'm still transfixed by the bee on my nose when I hear Madam Ada's voice. 'Put out your hand, Eliza,' she says. 'Just beside your nose.'

She dabs something yellow and sticky onto the top of my hand. The bee flies off my nose and lands on my hand where it stays, lapping up the honey. I start to feel a lot less nervous. In fact it's fun having a bee eating off your hand. I can see why Mama used to love it.

Madam Ada smiles. 'She likes you. Perhaps she recognises a Dublin neighbour. Her hive lives near Phoenix Park when she's not performing and during the rest of the year. Joseph is my trainee beekeeper. They perform for a few days and then they rest.'

Joseph works for the circus as a beekeeper? My mind is spinning. It all seems so unlikely and yet so perfect. Wait till Annie hears about all this!

Madam Ada watches the bee still happily lapping the honey from my hand. When another worker bee joins the first bee and then another until there are six bees on my hand, I don't flinch. I'm getting used to their tickly feet.

'Would you like a job while we're playing in Dublin, Eliza?' she asks. 'And your brother. Nothing glamorous, but the pay isn't bad. Mucking out the ring between performances with Albert, helping with my honeybees. Every afternoon between five and seven. It gets pretty busy between shows. Luca hurt his wrist during a tumble today and needs to rest it. Joseph can take over Luca's jobs but we could do with more hands. If your parents agree. You must ask them first of course.'

'Our Mama isn't here any more,' Jonty says. 'She got sick and, you know...' He tails off, not wanting to say the word.

'I'm sorry to hear that,' Madam Ada says gently.

I know Mama's death is not something he likes talking about so he quickly adds, 'Papa wouldn't mind, would he,

Eliza?' He looks at me hopefully. I'm not so sure, but I keep it to myself.

'I'm not all that good with animals,' I say instead. 'But Jonty is. He'd be much better at helping you with the bees.'

She nods at my hand. 'And yet it is you they have chosen,' she says. 'What do you say?'

'I say yes, yes, yes!' Jonty says. 'Please, Eliza? Papa needs money for his eye operation so this is perfect. Please say yes.' He looks so hopeful that I can't bear to disappoint him. It's been a tough year for Jonty and I know working with the circus animals would make him so happy.

And Jonty's right about needing the money. 'All right then,' I say. 'We'll try it, Madam Ada. I'm not sure how much use I'll be, but I promise to do my best.'

I'll need a bit of time to work out exactly how we can manage it. I know Papa won't approve. We'll have to keep it to ourselves for the moment and hope he doesn't find out. So I say, 'We'll come as soon as we can. It'll take me a few days to arrange it.'

Madam Ada smiles. '*Molto bene*. Your work will start at five o'clock sharp. If you could arrange overalls for our new helpers, Albert, I'd be most grateful.'

'Happy to, Aunt Ada,' Albert says. 'And welcome to the circus family,' Liza and Jonty.'

'Thanks, sis,' Jonty says. 'You're a brick.' He throws his arms around me and gives me the biggest hug ever. As I hug him back, I start to feel nervous. How on earth are we going to keep such an enormous secret from Papa? We can't just disappear for several hours every day with no explanation. Unless I can think of something Jonty's dreams will be dashed.

CHAPTER 15

*The worker bees look after their queen by feeding her royal jelly
produced by glands near their mouths.*

On Monday afternoon I dash out of the workshop and up the stairs, taking two at a time. Papa's a creature of habit: he likes eating lunch at midday and I'm a bit late. I've been painting Margaret-Anne's elephant all morning. Getting the right shade of grey – not too light and not too dark – is proving difficult. I have to build the colour up using thin layers of watercolour, letting each layer dry before adding another. It's a slow process and I lost all track of time.

When I burst through the door of our flat Papa's sitting at the table, tucking into what looks like some sort of pie.

'Papa?' I say, walking towards him.

He smiles up at me. 'Mr Pennefeather's butler appeared at the door at eleven with a basket of food. A pork pie, a glazed ham, even one of Sally's Apple Charlottes complete with a small pot of clotted cream. A feast fit for a king.'

He gestures at the table, which has been beautifully set for two. 'He insisted on setting the table for me. I'm sorry, my dear, I couldn't resist starting, I hope you'll forgive me.'

'Of course, Papa.' I'm still in shock at all the food on the table and on the sideboard. Sally was right, Mr Pennefeather really is generous.

'Sit down and join me,' he says. 'And I'd be grateful if you'd read me Mr Pennefeather's letter.' He points at the long white envelope resting against the water jug.

'Eat first,' he adds, 'then read. The pie is delicious. Bravo, Sally.'

He's right, it is. We both go quiet for the next few minutes as we savour the rich pastry and the tender meat inside, which is mixed with some sort of honey, cinnamon and apple chutney, so tasty.

When I've finished, feeling very full, I neatly line up my knife and fork in the middle of my plate and reach for the letter. I open the envelope, cracking Mr Pennefeather's circle of red sealing wax.

'*My Dearest Thomas,*' I begin to read out loud. Thomas is my father's name. '*I asked Sally to prepare some food for you. Please don't be angry, it's not charity, simply a gift from one friend to another. Or a little bit of a bribe I must admit.*

I do miss your company in the club, my friend, some of the members are such droning bores and I adore our political debates. I swear some of those oafs never touch a newspaper.

So I've had an idea. Please do me the very great honour of dining with me every Wednesday at midday in the King's Parlour at the club. Mr Dalton will collect you at half-past eleven and bring you home. Say yes, I beg you.'

I break off reading. 'What a kind offer. Will you go?'

Papa goes quiet for a moment, clearly torn. He loves talking to Mr Pennefeather. They used to spend hours in our sitting room in Rathmines discussing things like votes for women. Mama too when she was alive, she loved talking politics.

Papa and Mr Pennefeather both support the suffragettes, thank goodness – Mama was a devoted suffragette and would have turned them both out of the house otherwise – but they are a little more divided when it comes to nationalism.

Their most recent debate in Rathmines was about the upcoming royal visit. Mr Pennefeather is in favour of King George and Queen Mary's visit to Ireland in July, but Papa is not so sure. He believes Ireland should break away from

Britain and become a republic, with no monarch.

'Papa?' I ask again.

'It is a private room,' Papa says. 'No one would see me. And I do love his company.'

'Do go, Papa,' I say. 'It would cheer you up no end and I'm sure the food in the club is worth travelling for.'

'It is pretty special,' he admits. 'Their chef is from Paris.' He pauses. 'I'll think about it. Is there anything else in the letter?'

'Yes.' I read on. '*And I have a second favour to ask. Mr Stephens is very impressed with Jonty. Says he's a calming influence on my two tearaways. He was wondering if Jonty might stay a little later some days so they can all study together.*

I know it's a lot to ask, but it really would benefit Harry and Theo.

I do hope to see you next Wednesday at the club.

Your friend always,

Cedric'

'Papa,' I say, a plan starting to form in my head, 'the Pennefeathers have been so kind to Jonty, it's an excellent way for him to repay them. I can collect Jonty after study. And you must go to the club with Mr Pennefeather. Think of all the work I can get done on a Wednesday if I don't have to stop to prepare you luncheon.'

His face drops. 'Am I an awful burden, Eliza?'

'Not at all, Papa. But you do seem a little sad some days and dining with Mr Pennefeather would make you happy.'

He nods. 'You're right, it would make me happy. I'll go then. Can you write back to Mr Pennefeather? Tell him yes to the club and yes to borrowing Jonty to study with his boys. And perhaps we could make a special illuminated piece for him. Decorate one of his favourite poems to say thank you.'

'Of course, Papa. That's a lovely idea.' I smile to myself. I think Mr Pennefeather, bless him, might just have given me the answer to the circus dilemma. And I haven't seen Papa look so happy for a long time.

x x x

On Tuesday I arrive early at the Pennefeather's to arrange Jonty's extra study nights directly with Mr Stephens before class. I find him in the library. He's slim with round wire glasses and is a lot younger than I expected, about eighteen or nineteen. He's thrilled that Jonty will be joining Theo and Harry for study.

'They thump each other less when your brother's around,'

he says. 'He's the only thing keeping me here, to be honest. I've never met a boy more eager to learn science.'

I smile. 'Thanks, Mr Stephens, that's nice to hear.'

As I suspected, when I go back downstairs to tell Jonty he's less than thrilled.

'It's only twice a week, Jonty,' I tell him. 'Tuesdays and Thursdays, from tonight. You'll have to make your own way home later and meet me at the workshop at half-past seven so we can go up to the flat together. I'm supposed to be bringing you home, remember, but I'll be at the circus. Check the time on one of the clocks in the pawnshop windows on Rutland Square. But Papa thinks you're at the Pennefeathers' every evening so be careful. The other evenings you'll meet me up at the circus straight after class, got it?'

'I think so, but it's not fair! How come you get to go every day?'

'It's better than nothing, Jonty. And I don't even want to work at the circus, remember? I'm doing all this for you.'

'I suppose. It's still not fair though.'

X X X

All afternoon I work harder than I've ever worked before, determined to finish all Margaret-Anne's animals and get to the circus by five o'clock on the dot. I cannot wait!

At four o'clock I leave the workshop and go to the flat.

'Papa, I'm going to leave dinner on the table for you this evening. I'm going to go straight from the workshop to collect Jonty after study if that's ok. I'll get more work done that way.' I intend to leave his food out every evening in fact so I can get to the circus on time.

He smiles at me. 'You're a good girl, Eliza. I'm really proud of you.'

It makes me feel a little guilty, to be honest. I don't like lying to him but I have to.

And so our new life with the circus begins.

CHAPTER 16

Bees transport a plant's pollen from flower to flower. The pollen
sticks to the hairs on their hind legs and they pack it
into their 'pollen sacs', small bowl-like indents
on their back legs.

As I walk towards the circus compound I have knots in my stomach. I regret making Jonty study with the Pennefeathers this evening. I'd be much more confident if he was here beside me. He's the one who is good with animals. He's the one everyone likes. Not me!

This is a bad idea. A very bad idea. I'm about to turn on my heel and run home when I hear my name. Or a version of my name.

"Liza, that you? Over 'ere!'

It's Albert, waving from the steps of one of the caravans to the far left of the big top. He jumps down and walks towards me, Pepper and Miss Primrose at his heels.

'Good to see you, matey,' he says, slapping my back. 'All set for some dung action? I was saving it up until you showed. Figured it would make a rubbish job a bit more fun if we attacked it together.'

I give as bright a smile as I can manage. 'All set,' I say.

'Don't be nervous, bunch of misfits and outsiders all of us. You'll slot right in.'

I think about this for a second. Is he calling me a misfit?

But he gives a huge grin. 'Your face! I'm joking. Aunt Ada sent these over. You can use my caravan to change in.' He hands me a pair of dark green boy's overalls. I stare at them.

'I can't wear those. Girls don't wear trousers.'

He shrugs. 'Some girls do. Coco wears them all the time. Look.' He points over at Coco who is practising a tumbling trick on the grass beside the horses. Sure enough, she's wearing black tweed trousers held up by braces.

'I'm not sure Coco owns a dress, mind,' he adds.

Then I spot Lulu wearing exactly the same dark green overalls as the ones in my hands. She's with Franco by the main tent. They're each swinging large wooden mallets and knocking the tent pegs further into the ground. I watch them for a moment, as the mallets go whack, whack, whack against the wood.

It reminds me of Mama. She used to cut the long grass at the bottom of our garden with a scythe, swinging it from side to side with a loud swishing noise, the curved blade slicing through the grass.

I remember one day in particular. Papa was sitting in a deck chair, reading his newspaper and I was sprawled on a rug beside him, reading a book.

'Darn skirt!' Mama said. She put down the scythe, gathered up the middle of her skirt and tucked it into her belt, so it looked like baggy bloomers.

'You're the height of fashion, Melissa,' Papa told her with a laugh, peering at her over his *Irish Times*. 'I've been reading about the new trouser skirts they're wearing in Paris right here. All the rage apparently. Suits you. Might get a pair myself.'

'You should, Thomas. And you're welcome to wear one of my skirts any time you like. Then you'd find out gardening in them is a nuisance.'

Thinking about it, Mama would definitely approve of work overalls for girls.

'I'll wear them,' I tell Albert. As I walk up the caravan steps I hitch up my skirt so I don't trip. My sketchbook falls out of my skirt pocket and tumbles down the steps towards Albert. He picks it up.

'What's this?' he asks with interest. He's about to open the cover when I say, 'Stop! That's private.'

The tops of his ears go bright red. 'Sorry, didn't mean to upset you. I was just curious, that's all.'

'No, I'm sorry, Albert. I didn't mean to snap. It's my sketch-book.'

'Can I see?'

I nod a little. 'All right. But they're not very good. My drawings I mean.'

He flicks through the pages. 'Not good? Are you mad, 'Liza? They're only bloomin' brilliant.' He turns the book around to show me the page he's looking at. 'You've captured Rex perfectly. And hang on, is that me?' He points at a drawing of himself dancing with Pepper.

This time it's my turn to go red. 'Yes. Now, I'd better get changed.' I put my hand down to take the sketchbook back. Then I put it safely in my pocket, walk into the caravan and close the split door behind me, top and bottom.

For a moment I just stand there, taking it all in, the brightly painted wood of the walls – sunny yellow, grass green and cherry red. The ceiling is decorated with the most amazing life-like flowers, roses, poppies and peonies. Whoever painted them is a really talented artist.

There's a small iron stove to the left and a built-in red velvet sofa on the opposite wall, and at the back of the caravan is a raised bed covered in a patchwork eiderdown. On the narrow windowsill are a row of tiny dogs carved from wood, no bigger than my thumb. Albert is so lucky! It's a cosy slice of heaven.

'You all right in there, 'Liza?' he calls from outside.

'Yes, nearly ready.' I stop looking around and lift the silver locket Mama gave me for my thirteenth birthday off my shirt and tuck it carefully under the neck of the shirt, against my skin. There's a picture of her and Papa inside and I never take it off, not if I can help it. Then I quickly unbutton my shirt and pull it over my head. My skirt is next. Then I sit on the sofa in my cotton shift and drawers and pull on the overalls, one leg at a time.

Buttoning up the overalls I feel a rush of excitement. I smile to myself. It's the first time I've ever worn trousers. But that's nothing compared to my first day working in the circus. Me, Eliza Kane, working for a circus. Imagine!

I spend the next hour shovelling horse dung and lion droppings from the ring and throwing down fresh sawdust. You haven't met stinky until you've met lion poo!

It's hard work and the opposite of glamorous, but I love every minute of it, especially with Albert to keep me company. Time passes quickly as we chat and joke around.

'Odour *de* mucking out,' he says, giving a huge sniff as we fork the last of the dung from the wheelbarrow to the dung heap at the very corner of the field where the horses are gambolling. A market farmer comes to collect it once a week, Albert told me. He uses it as manure for his vegetables.

'Ripe and pungent,' Albert continues, 'with a lingering after-smell of rotting sawdust. *Parfait.*' He pinches his fingers together, touches them to his lips and kisses them with a loud smacking noise, like a French chef. 'Does *mademoiselle* agree?'

'*Oui, bien sûr,*' I say. '*L'odeur est magnifique.*'

He stops forking and stares at me. 'Here, do you speak French, 'Liza? Yer accent is sound as a pound.'

I smile. '*Un petit peu.* Mama was a French teacher. And half-French herself.'

He whistles. 'I'm impressed. She must be one smart lady,

your mum.'

'She was,' I say, forking up another lump of dung to avoid his eyes. 'Very smart.'

'Of course, she's gone, isn't she?' he says gently. 'Jonty said before. Mine too. I'm an orphan. The circus folk are my family now. You have any family apart from Jonty?'

'Just Papa. He was an artist and ran a printers but his eyesight is very bad now so he can't work. What happened to your parents, if you don't mind me asking?'

'Don't mind at all.' Albert tips the wheelbarrow and most of the dung falls onto the heap. 'Hold the barrow tipped will you, 'Liza and I'll scrape out the last bits. Nearly done then.'

'So my parents,' he continues, raising his voice a little over the scraping. 'Never knew my da. Died when I was a nipper. Diphtheria did for my ma. I was already working with the circus at that stage. Aunt Ada had spotted me busking with Pepper and Miss Primrose. Some circus folk have a problem with jossers, but not Aunt Ada.'

'What's a josser?' I ask.

'An outsider. Not born into the circus like Zozimus. His father, Zozimus Senior, was ringmaster before him. Retired to Cornwell with the missus last year, but they travel with us from time to time when they get the itch.'

'And Madam Ada? Was she born into the circus?'

'You're joking, right? Aunt Ada comes from money, a lot of it from all accounts. She grew up in Milan and her father's some sort of posh Italian lord or something. Disinherited her when she ran off and joined the circus. She was in London singing in an opera and met Zozimus at a fancy party. It was love at first sight apparently. For Zozimus anyway.'

'How romantic!' I say.

Albert shrugs. 'Suppose it is.'

He wipes the prongs of the fork on the grass and I do the same with mine. 'Worst job of the day done, thanks to your help, 'Liza. Usually takes me twice as long.' He starts wheeling the wheelbarrow back towards the tents and I walk beside him.

'How long have you been travelling with the circus?' I ask.

'Since just before my fourteenth birthday. I'll be fifteen in July, so almost a year.' He stops for a second. 'I feel older than fourteen sometimes. Ma getting sick and losing her and all that lark, it weren't much fun. Don't know what I would have done without Aunt Ada and Zozimus.' He shakes himself. 'Woah, too serious, Albert. Anyhows, I'm not complaining.

I've a good life with the circus. Couldn't think of a better way to spend my days. And you can tell me all about your life while we do our next job. Believe me, we'll need distraction.'

'What is the next job?'

'Brushing Rex's mane. It gets really knotty and you have to pull quite hard.'

'What?' I stare at him; his face is stony serious. But then it cracks and he bursts into laughter.

'Kidding! We need to brush the dogs. Far safer.'

I punch the top of his arm. 'Albert! I can't believe I fell for that.'

'I think a gnat landed on my arm.'

I punch him again, harder.

'Nah, maybe it was a fly.'

And again.

'All right, all right, keep your cool, 'Liza.' He takes off at speed towards the caravans, the wheelbarrow bumping over the grass.

'Albert, the forks,' I call after him.

'All yours,' he calls back. 'That's what you get for the little mouse thumps.'

X X X

We're sitting on the steps of his caravan, brushing Princess Ellie and Salty when Madam Ada walks towards us.

'Bee wagon time,' Albert says. 'You go inside and change out of them overalls, 'Liza. You won't need them where we're going next. There's a wash pitcher and basin on the sideboard. Fresh water for you and all.'

'Thanks, Albert.'

I wash my hands and change back into my clothes. Hopefully the lingering smell of dung will have worn off by the time I get home.

'Fresh as a daisy,' Albert says as I come back out.

'What will I do with these?' I nod at the overalls in my hand.

'They're yours now,' he says. 'I'll hang them up to be aired for tomorrow. How did it feel, wearing trousers for the first time?'

I smile. 'Magic! Wish I could wear them all the time.'

CHAPTER 17

Flowers of edible plants like apples, raspberries and cucumbers can only become fruit or vegetables if the flower is pollinated. That is why bees are so important.

'These *beautiful* honeybees have worked hard,' Madam Ada says as Albert and I help her carefully load three hives into the back of the red wagon. 'Now they are going home for a few days' rest before they perform again.'

'Are the Queens inside the hives?' I ask, remembering the little cage from yesterday.

'They certainly are,' she says. 'Without its own Queen, a bee community won't function. Every hive has a Queen; she lays eggs which produce new bees. Worker bees, drones and new Queens.'

'The bees won't fly out while we travel?' I ask.

She smiles. 'Good question. There's a wire mesh over the hive doors to stop them. So you will not need a veil or gloves as they will be inside their hives the whole way. Albert will ride up in front with me. Will you fetch Star and bridle him up, Albert?'

'Aye, aye, Captain.' Albert tips his hand to his head in a salute and walks off towards the horses.

'You'll ride in the back with the bees, Eliza,' Madam Ada says. 'Your job is to sing to them when they seem agitated.' I look at her face carefully. Is she joking about singing to them, like Albert saying we were to brush Rex's mane? I don't want to get caught out again. But no, she seems perfectly serious.

'How will I know if they're agitated?' I ask.

She smiles. 'Oh, you will know.'

'What kind of songs do they like?' I ask.

'Lullabies,' she says with a smile, as if singing to bees was the most natural thing in the world.

X X X

We rumble along King Street towards Phoenix Park, home of the Zoological Gardens. It used to be one of Mama's favourite places to walk and picnic.

We hit a pothole and the wagon jolts, sending the bees into a tizzy. They buzz loudly and angrily.

Madam Ada turns around and smiles at me. 'Time to charm the bees, Eliza. Try talking to them first. If that doesn't work, sing. The words don't matter, it's the tone they react to. Keep it calm and soothing.'

I start taking to the hives, feeling ridiculous. 'Sorry about the bump, bees. I know you're not fleas, or chimpanzees. You don't like jumping as you don't have knees. Not proper knees. What else rhymes with bees? Sneeze? Disease? No, that's not a good one.'

I ignore Albert's gleeful chuckles at my nonsense. I ignore him and carry on.

'I know you want to be home, sucking nectar, little bees, and not being bounced around, but we're nearly there. And we haven't met a bear. Or a square. Or a hare.'

Albert bursts into laughter.

I'm not sure it's working, they're still buzzing away.

'Keep going, Eliza,' Madam Ada says. 'You're doing very well. Pay no attention to Albert. Turn around, Albert, and stop bothering her!'

We drive over another even larger pothole and this time the hives lift off the floor and smack down again. The bees start buzzing so noisily that the hives are practically levitating.

'Time to sing, Eliza,' Madam Ada says. 'Loud as you can.

We're nearly at Stoneybatter.'

I remember what she said about lullabies so I break into 'Hush, little bees, don't say a word, Mama's going to buy you a mockingbird. If that mockingbird don't sing, Mama's going to buy you a diamond ring.' It's one Mama used to sing to us at bedtime.

When I've finished that one I try another of Mama's songs, a French one called '*Au clair de la lune*'. Then I sing 'All is well, bees, all is well. Go to sleep, bees, go to sleep' to the tune of Brahms' lullaby.

The next thing I know the bees have stopped buzzing and the wagon has also stopped, in front of tall black wooden gates.

Madam Ada swings around in her seat. She gives me a beautiful smile which makes her whole face light up. 'Bravo, *Stellina*. You have a beautiful voice and that was remarkable. You charmed the bees and also this young man from the look of things. I've never known him to be so still and quiet. He's normally Mr Fidget.'

For once, Albert says nothing and the tips of his ears go pink. He jumps down from his seat and says, 'Hand me the key, Aunt Ada, and I'll open up for you. And she's right, I liked your singing, 'Liza.'

I smile at him, feeling my own cheeks blush. 'Thanks, Albert.'

CHAPTER 18

When a honeybee is flying it moves its wings so fast that the air
around it starts to vibrate. This creates the buzzing
noise that we can hear.

I'm so full to bursting with circus and bee news to tell Jonty,
I practically skip the whole way back to Henrietta Street. I'm
about to run up the stairs of number sixteen towards our flat
when I remember that I'd arranged to meet him at the workshop, so I go out the back door into the yard instead.

I'm delighted to see Annie washing cups and plates under
the yard tap. I'm getting used to the mud out here and the
stench of the closets and the pigs. The yard doesn't seem so
scary any more, but I still won't go near it at night. Not with
the rats, no way!

I see them practically every day, scuttling along the walls
looking for food, mostly when it's getting dark. I stood on a
'clock' getting out of bed this morning, that's what they call
cockroaches in the tenements. It crunched under my heel

and when I jumped back in fright it ran away. Horrible, horrible creatures!

'Hey, Annie!' I call. I walk towards her, hopping over some pony droppings that no one has bothered cleaning up.

'You're a sight for sore eyes.' She clunks the battered white enamel mug she's washing into the bucket and dries her hands on her apron. 'Tenement china. All done until tomorrow. Feels like my hands are in water from dawn to dusk some days. Like a fish.'

'Or a beautiful mermaid,' I say. 'Full of secrets and mysteries.'

'You're in a good mood I see.' She grins and then the smile falls off her face. 'Here, I don't mean to be rude, but the pong off you, Eliza. You been mucking out the pony or something?'

I laugh. 'You've a good nose. It's manure all right, but not pony, horse. White stallions in fact. I haven't had a chance to tell you, but I'm helping at the circus every day after work. With Albert, he's from London and he's ever so funny. He trains all the performing dogs. The circus is up in the fields behind the Black Church. First we mucked out the ring, that took ages, then we brought Madam Ada's bees back home to-'

Annie puts both hands up. 'Woah there, Eliza. Circus? When did all this happen? And what about the animal drawings you're supposed to be working on? Is your old man all right with all this circus lark?'

I go quiet for a moment.

'You haven't told him, have you?' she says. It must be written all over my face. 'Eliza, you big eejit. He's going to go mad when he finds out. And then it's goodbye circus.'

'How's he going to find out? You're not going to tell him, are you?' The thought of leaving the circus makes me physically shiver.

'Course not,' Annie says. 'But if you go upstairs reeking of horses and gabbling and bubbling like you've been to the best party in the land he'll figure out something's up. From what you tell me he's no fool. You have to be careful, that's all.'

'Sorry, Annie, I didn't mean to snap at you. The thought of not seeing Albert and all the animals again, I couldn't bear it. It's the best thing that's ever happened to me.'

'I'm still confused,' Annie says. 'Tell me how you ended up as a circus stable girl. Slowly. Start at the beginning.'

So I tell her all about Jonty saving Pepper, the circus show and our ringside seats and Madam Ada asking us to work for her.

She smiles. 'I can see why you're so excited. May as well enjoy it while you can. But you have to wash, Eliza. Stick your head under the tap and I'll help you rinse the pong out of your hair. And I'll give you a mob cap to keep it clean tomorrow.'

She leans forwards and sniffs my dress. 'Your clothes seem all right, but the state of your boots.' I look down. She's right, they're covered in muck from the horses and grass from Madam Ada's bee garden. I'm about to say I have another pair I can work in, but I stop myself. I think Annie only has one pair of boots.

'I'll clean them,' I say, twisting the tap on and sticking each boot under the water in turn, bending down and rubbing at the leather with my hand to take off the worst of the dirt.

Then Annie helps me wash my hair with Sunlight soap. The water is cold and it makes my scalp tingle, but it does the trick: most of the horsey smell has gone. Afterwards Annie takes off her apron and hands it to me.

'Here, dry your hair with this. Don't worry, it's clean. Then we'll fetch you that mob cap.'

'Thanks, Annie.' After I've dried my hair off a bit and it stops dripping we go in the back door and up the stairs towards her flat.

Raven, the McAllister's cat, runs across the yard in front of us and I suddenly remember – Tall Joe!

'You'll never guess who I bumped into working at the circus,' I say. 'Only Tall Joe. And guess what he called you? My Annie.'

Annie stops dead and stares at me. 'At the circus? Wonder why he didn't tell me? And did he really say that? Are you sure? Tell me exactly what he said, Eliza, every word.'

When I've finished filling her in, she blows out her breath. 'Well I never.' She presses her hands against her pink cheeks.

'He's definitely soft on you, Annie.'

She shrugs, but I can see she's pleased. 'He's a daft sod, and no mistake,' she says.

'But he's your daft sod.'

'I suppose he is. Come on, let's get be getting that cap for you.' We walk in the back door together and up the stairs.

Annie stands outside her door for a moment, her hand on the door knob. 'Eliza, it's not like your place. We don't have much in the way of furniture. But it's clean as a new pin.'

'I'm sure it's lovely,' I say.

She says nothing, simply opens the door and I instantly feel guilty. It's not at all like our flat. It's a large room with a high ceiling and two tall sash windows overlooking the street. Many of the window panes are broken and covered with pieces of cardboard. Some of the panes at the top are missing completely. It's fine now in June when the air isn't too cold, but it must be freezing in the winter.

The bare floorboards are all cracked and bockety. In one corner, to the right of the fireplace, practically a whole plank is missing. Newspaper has been stuffed into the hole, to stop the draughts. The walls, once sky blue, are now battered and faded and there seems to be some sort of black mould inching across the ceiling.

There's a battered old pine dresser on the left-hand wall beside the fireplace, with a framed photograph of a dark haired, serious-looking woman staring out. It must be Annie's mother. In the corner is an empty slop bucket, but as soon as I spot it I pull my eyes away immediately. There's something too personal and private about it to stare. We have one too, but ours is hidden during the day behind a folding screen.

Between the two windows there's a small rickety wooden table with one equally rickety chair and stool.

But it's the beds that get to me. Or the lack of them. There's one ancient-looking single iron bed pushed against the far right-hand wall with a thin, stained brown mattress on it and along the back wall are two lumpy looking mattresses on the floor. Someone – Annie probably – has stitched together flour bags and stuffed them with straw. There are old, torn and patched tweed coats laid carefully at the end of the beds. I wonder what they are doing there until I realise they must be Annie and her brother's blankets. Six of them sleeping on these make-shift 'beds' on the floor!

I'm so overcome with guilt at what I have – my own comfy brass bed, a quilt to keep me warm, rugs, furniture, spare boots, books – that I almost start to cry.

'Now don't be going all funny on me,' Annie says. 'I'm not ashamed of how we live, don't go making me ashamed, understand? It won't always be like this. George and Sid will be old enough to get jobs and look after themselves one day, and once they're all set up I can go into service full time. Any big house would be lucky to have me.' She tilts up her chin.

'It would,' I agree. 'I'm sorry. I just didn't...' I tail off.

'Know we were so poor? We're not, compared to some, like the families in Henrietta Cottages.' She shrugs. 'Thought you might not want to be friends with me if you knew the truth.'

'Annie! That's a terrible thing to say.'

She lifts her eyebrows. 'You had tenement friends before moving here, did you?'

'No,' I say honestly. It's something I've been thinking about a lot since seeing my so-called college friends at College Green. I realise now if they really cared about me they would have waited to say 'hello' and to find out how I was.

'I didn't really have any friends at all,' I say, 'not best friends anyway. There are a few girls in college I like, but I find them hard to talk to sometimes. It's not like talking to you. I feel like I can say anything to you, be myself. Does that make sense?'

She looks at me, her eyes soft. 'It does. Best friends, eh? I like that. I've never had one neither.' She smiles at me and I smile back.

I nod. 'Best friends.'

She pulls open a drawer in the dresser and takes out something white. 'Here. Mob cap. It's my spare one. Have to wear them for my cleaning jobs.'

She hands it to me and I stare down at it, a baggy, floppy cotton cap with elastic around the edges. A maid's cap.

Time for more honesty. 'I know it's a good idea, Annie, and I'm really grateful as I don't have time to wash my hair every day, but it will look daft with my green mucking-out overalls.'

To my relief she laughs. She takes it off me and puts it back in the dresser. 'That it will. Does Jonty have a cap?'

'He did, but he's lost it.'

She walks over to the back of the door where two boys' caps are hanging on nails and hands me the larger one, brown tweed.

'It's George's,' she says. 'He won't mind. If you put your hair up and stick this over the top it'll do the trick.' She twists my hair gently and carefully into a loose chignon and plonks the cap on my head before my hair has time to unravel.

'Suits you!' she says.

Tears spring to my eyes. I blink them away. 'Sorry,' I mumble, embarrassed.

'What's wrong, Eliza?'

'Once I turned twelve Mama used to plait my hair every morning. She has – had – gentle hands, like yours. No one's touched my hair since then.'

'Ah, pet,' Annie puts her arms around me and gives me a big hug. 'I miss my mam too. Only natural.' She pulls back and gently wipes my tears away with her fingers. 'It'll get easier, I promise.'

The door flies open and we look over. George is standing in the doorway with Jonty beside him. Oops, I'd forgotten all about Jonty.

Jonty glares at me. 'You said you'd meet me in the work-shop after study. I waited for ages. George said he'd seen you talking to Annie in the yard. And why are you wearing that stupid cap?'

'My cap,' George says, although he seems more curious than cross.

'Eliza needs it for work,' Annie says. 'To keep her head warm when she's drawing.'

George seems to accept this. 'Fine, she can borrow it. You look like a boy though, Eliza.'

'Good lad,' Annie says. 'Now, go back downstairs and tell Sid it's time to practise his reading and writing. You too. Say goodbye to Jonty now, please.'

'All right,' George says. 'Bye, Jonty. Slave driver has us doing extra school work every night.' He gives a groan.

'I have to study practically every night too,' Jonty says with a sigh. 'Eliza's fault.'

'Sisters, eh?' George says with a wink. 'Who'd have 'em?'

'Too right,' Jonty says.

'See you tomorrow, Jonty,' George says, running out the door.

'Charming, aren't they?' Annie says, lifting her eyebrows at me. 'We work our fingers to the bone and there's gratitude for you. In fact George would spend his whole day drawing if I gave him half a chance. Loves it. Like you, Eliza. Now, inside here for a minute, Jonty. You don't need all the neighbours knowing your business.' She lowers her voice. 'Or your father for that matter.'

Jonty comes inside and she closes the door. He doesn't seem at all surprised by the room. Perhaps he's been inside before or maybe he simply doesn't notice the lack of furniture.

'Sorry for forgetting about you, Jonty,' I say.

He scowls at me and says nothing.

'You didn't say anything to George about the circus, did you?' Annie asks Jonty.

'No,' he says. 'Eliza said I wasn't to tell a soul.'

'Good. He might accidentally tell one of the other boys and it might get back to your father. But me, on the other hand, I want to hear more about what you got up to today, Eliza.' She grins. 'It's one the most exciting thing I've ever heard. You said something about bees.'

'We visited the circus' garden near Phoenix Park with Madam Ada,' I explain. 'She's the bee charmer and that's where her Dublin bees live.'

'I had to do mathematics while you saw a bee garden?' Jonty says. 'So unfair!'

'And aren't you lucky to be helping at the circus at all?'

Annie says. 'George and Sid would give their eye teeth to be you right now, Jonty. Right, all the details, Eliza, quick, before the boys get back. And she's said she's sorry, Jonty, so you can take that sour puss off your face. Go on, Eliza.'

I tell her all about the trip in the wagon and singing to the bees – Jonty made me tell that bit twice – and then the Honey Garden.

'I don't know how to describe it,' I say. 'It was like something out of a fairy tale. As soon as Albert opened the gates and we drove in, the smell, like a beautiful perfume factory. Roses and honeysuckle and this special kind of heather that the bees love. There's a path through the flowers for the wagon to reach the hives. They're all along the back wall, a dozen of them, like a village of little white wooden houses with hundreds of bees flying in and out of them. The air's alive with bees!

'There's cherry trees and red maples and a pond with lily pads and huge Japanese goldfish swimming in it – carp Albert said – and a red wooden pagoda beside it with a curvy roof, that's a fancy oriental garden house. There's a matching red bench in it with lions' heads on the back, really fancy.'

'Sounds beautiful,' Annie says. 'I'd love to visit it one day.'

'It is,' I say. 'I'll ask Madam Ada, I'm sure she wouldn't mind. Tall Joe looks after the bees, maybe he'll take you one day.'

Is it my imagination or do her cheeks go a little pink?

'If the flowers smelled so good, why do you stink so bad?' Jonty asks.

'Jonty!' I say. 'Annie's just spent the last while helping me wash.'

'Sorry, Annie,' Jonty says. 'I'm sure you did your best but she's still a bit stinky. Don't worry, I'll say it's all the strange food at the Pennefeathers. Left-over pheasant I had to eat today, disgusting! I'll tell Papa I let off a rotten egg ripper if he asks about the smell.'

I laugh. 'Thanks, Jonty, that's really kind of you.'

'I can practice if you like,' he says.

'No!' Annie and I say together.

But it's too late, he's already scrunched up his face and let out a noisy parp.

'Jonty, please,' I say. 'Stop being so rude.'

Annie grins. 'I'm well used to it with my two brothers. Boys are disgusting!'

X X X

Papa doesn't say anything about my smell, thank goodness. After talking to him, I clear up the mess he made preparing himself dinner, trying not to sigh.

His water glass is on its side and there are soggy crumbs all over the table and water on the floor. He must have knocked it over. I know it's not his fault but it's still annoying.

After grabbing a piece of bread for my own dinner, I get Jonty washed and to bed before finally sitting down at the desk in the workshop by lamp light. Even though the muscles in my arms are aching from lifting all that manure with the fork – it's surprisingly heavy – I manage to finish Margaret-Anne's birthday hymn.

It's almost midnight before I stagger up the stairs, bone weary, and flop into bed.

CHAPTER 19

The queen bee usually lives for around three or four years, but she may live for up to seven. The queen bee produces a special scent that the other bees can smell.

On Friday I walk quickly down Dorset Street to meet Jonty on the corner of Granby Row at half-past four as we'd arranged.

When he spots me he says 'Come on, slow coach! I don't want to be late for my first day at the circus.' He starts sprinting towards Black Church Fields.

I run after him but halfway up Granby Row my legs are so tired I have to stop.

'Jonty,' I yell after him. 'Wait!'

He stops, turns around and runs back towards me, a big scowl on his face.

'Can't you go faster, Eliza?'

'I'm doing my best. Look, you go on if you like. Tell them I'm on my way. You'll be faster without me.'

'Circus, here I come,' he says, taking off again. I watch as he weaves in and out of the pedestrians on the pavement, getting smaller and smaller. In a few moments he's the size of an ant and then he disappears.

I can't remember ever feeling this tired before. I can't manage any more running but I walk as fast as I can.

When I get to Black Church Fields the first person I see is Tall Joe, bashing the circus tent pegs with a wooden mallet, his body folded over like the letter R. Wood hitting wood with a hollow tok, tok, tok.

'Hello, Tall Joe.'

He straightens up and smiles at me. 'Greetings, Eliza. Good to see you again. Jonty's with Albert. They're doing mad things with the dogs. How are you feeling after all the manure lugging over the last few days?'

'A bit stiff to be honest but I'll get used to it. Can I ask you something? Annie was surprised to hear about your circus job. How long have you been working here?'

'Four years, on and off. Every June I pack in my work on the docks and come and help Madam Ada while the circus is in town. The thought of it keeps me going all year. I love it.' He sweeps his long arm around and smiles at the circus tent. 'I'm never happier than when I'm with my circus family. I'll spend the rest of my life at the docks, and that's all right, I can deal with that as long as I get my break with the circus every year.

'Sorry if I landed you in it with Annie. Thought it best not to say anything to her. They've always taken me back at the docks come July, but it is a bit of a risk and Annie's a bit risk averse, what with her father and all.'

I must look puzzled because he adds 'You know, anti-risk. It might help if he gave Annie his wages instead of drinking them in The Workman's Arms. Her older brothers aren't much better either. She looks after George and Sid pretty much all by herself.'

'Poor Annie,' I say. 'I had no idea.'

'Look, don't tell Annie I said anything. I'm sure Mr O'Hanlon does his best.'

I've never actually met Mr O'Hanlon. From what Tall Joe's saying that's not surprising if he spends most of his time in the pub. And it might explain the stumbling noises and loud singing I sometimes hear on the stairs late at night.

'I won't,' I say. 'I'm sure she'll understand about the circus job if you explain. She just wants you to be happy.'

'Do you think so?'

I nod vigorously. Yes!'

He smiles. 'I will, so. I was thinking of asking her to step out with me this Sunday. Madam Ada's given me the afternoon off. A walk around St Stephen's Green Park and tea and sticky buns in Bewley's Oriental Café – what do you think? Would Annie like that or is it a bit la-di-da?'

'She'd love it. Do ask her, as soon as you get back to Henrietta Street.' He still looks a bit uncertain, so I add, 'Don't tell her I said anything but I know she's very fond of you. I'm sure she'll say yes.'

His ears go bright red and he grins back at me. 'I'll ask her, so. Tomorrow after work. Need to scrub up first and I promised the nippers I'd play footie with them this evening. Thanks, Eliza. You've made my day. And it's Joseph by the way. That's what my friends and family call me. And we're going to be great friends, me and you, I can tell.'

I smile at him. What a lovely thing to say. 'I do hope so, Joseph.'

As I walk away, I hear him whistling a jaunty tune in between the tock, tock, tock of the mallet.

X X X

Joseph was right, Albert and Jonty *are* doing mad things with the dogs. Jonty is trying to put what looks like a tiny white boxing glove on one of Salty's paws, but Salty's having none of it, pulling it off with his teeth and running around the grass with it in his mouth.

'What on earth are you doing?' I ask Albert, who is watching Jonty chase after Salty.

"Liza, me old pal!' He smiles at me, his eyes twinkling. 'Aunt Ada's looking for you. And we are trying to teach the boxer to box of course.'

'Right,' I say. 'Because dogs love boxing, do they?'

He laughs. 'Not this one. I think I'll have to try teaching Miss Primrose instead.'

'How's Jonty getting on?'

'Magic, the dogs love him.'

'Good, tell him I'm here and I'll see him later. Where will I find Madam Ada?'

'At the bee wagon.' He points left, towards the side of the horse field. 'Hope you're in the mood for some bee charming.'

As I walk towards the wagon I can hear Madam Ada singing, her voice soaring up, up, up, notes so high they touch the sky. She has a beautiful voice. Mama once told me that some opera singers can shatter a wine glass with their high notes. I wonder if Madam Ada's ever tried it.

I stand in front of the wagon, listening. All I can see is the back of Madam Ada's head. She's sitting in the wagon with the hives, leaning against the wooden tailboard, the tips of her elbows pointing towards me.

As I watch, a stream of bees leaves one of the hives and forms an aerial halo around her head. Then another stream appears from the hive and flies towards me.

'Sing to them, *Stellina*,' Madam Ada says without turning around. 'Do you know any more French songs? You sing so beautifully in French.'

Normally my head would be full of questions and I wouldn't be afraid to ask them, like how do you know it's me behind you? Why do you call me "*Stellina*"?

But right now a feeling of peace comes over me and I focus on the bees. I can ask questions later.

It's like what happens when I'm focused on my drawing and everything else falls away. At this moment it's just me and the bees.

I start to sing the French lullaby Mama taught me. '*Au*

clair de la lune, mon ami Pierrot …' I make it as gentle and as lyrical as I can. I forget some of the words and hum those bits instead.

'*Bonne nuit, cher trésor, Ferme tes yeux et dors. Laisse ta tête, s'envoler, Au creux de ton oreiller.*'

I start to make up some of my own words in English. 'Close your eyes, little bees. You are like little treasures. Rubies and pearls, silver and gold, you fly though the sky.'

The bees weave around my head, so close I can hear the throb of their wings and almost feel their furry bodies brush against my skin. One lands on my cheek and this time I don't stiffen or flinch. I let her rest there until she flies away.

When I've finished the song there's a long hush. I close my eyes for a moment and take in the silence. I haven't felt so calm and untroubled for such a long time. Not since before Mama got sick.

We used to lie on a rug under the oak tree in the garden, my head on her skirts. She'd sing to me, gently stroking my hair. 'Close your eyes, Eliza,' she'd whisper. 'What do you hear?'

'Nothing,' I'd say.

'Listen again. Listen harder.'

So I would. Then I'd say 'The wind rustling the leaves. Birds singing. A bee buzzing.'

'That's right, Eliza. Learn to be still and nature will unfold all its magic.'

Madam Ada turns around and smiles at me, breaking me out of my memories. '*Stellina*, you have the gift. You are a bee charmer. Where did you learn that beautiful song?'

'My mother. She died last December. Just before Christmas.'

Madam Ada's eyes rest on mine. I notice tiny specks of hazel flecking the green of her eyes. Such eyes! Like deep lakes.

'Ah, yes,' she says. 'I remember your brother mentioning it. I am sorry. I also have experienced great loss. It is never easy. You must miss her dreadfully. Albert said she was a teacher. Clearly a woman of many talents.'

I nod, unable to say anything else.

'And would you also like to teach, *Stellina*?'

I shake my head. 'No, I'd like to be an artist one day. Maybe.'

She smiles. 'Albert said you love to draw.'

'He seems to have told you a lot about me,' I say.

She laughs. 'He likes you, *Stellina*. And I myself find you a most fascinating girl. Tonight my favourite Queen will help me perform in the ring, Queen Regina. I will place her around my neck and she will call her hive to join me in the ring. I have a special request. I would like you to draw her for me. A portrait of my Queen Regina.'

X X X

I thought sketching a bee would be difficult, that she would jiggle around and then fly away before I could capture her likeness on paper. But Queen Regina seems perfectly happy to sit on the back of Madam Ada's hand, lapping sugar water.

I try to give Queen Regina's portrait as much detail as I can, capturing the soft fur on her back and her legs, and the delicate skeleton of her wings. I get lost in the drawing, carefully hatching and shading, smudging and highlighting. I don't want to disappoint Madam Ada.

Finally, happy that I've made the drawing as good as I can, I tear it out of my sketchbook carefully and hand it to her. 'For you,' I say.

Madam Ada gazes at the sketch for several minutes – making me squirm with nerves - before lifting her head. '*Bellissimo*. You have truly captured Regina's spirit. It doesn't just look like her, it feels like her. That is a remarkable gift. You have a great talent, *Stellina*. You must not squander it. There is no maybe about it. You *must* be an artist.'

'That's what my friend Annie says,' I say, staring down at my hands.

'Why so glum, *piccola*? Talent is a magical thing.'

'I was in art college and I miss it. My father can't see, so I have to work and look after my brother too. I'd love to go back to art college and become an artist, but I'm not sure how that's going to happen.'

'I understand, but don't give up on your dreams. The universe is full of surprises.' She shrugs. 'If I can run off and join the circus, you can become an artist. You must be strong. Becoming an artist won't be easy, especially for a girl. Your Mama must have studied very hard to become a teacher, that was not an easy path to take for a woman. I think you too are *una ragazza coraggiosa*, a brave girl.'

There's a loud roar from one of the lions and I jump a little, breaking the tension.

She pats my hand. 'Karina's girls are ready for their dinner. Think about what I said, *Stellina*. In a few years you'll be all grown up. Just like that.' She snaps her fingers. 'If you wish to be an artist, be brave and fight for it.'

There's another roar.

She smiles. 'Enough lectures for one day. I'll put Queen Regina's portrait on my wall and then you can draw the big cats eating.'

x x x

As I watch the cats ripping through their dinner – and boy, can they wolf it down, they're far worse than Jonty – I think about what Madam Ada said. She's right about Mama. She must have worked really hard to become a teacher. But what if I don't have Mama's drive and determination? What if I'm not brave enough?

I take my sketchbook out of my pocket and start drawing the lions. Within seconds my mind is calm and I'm lost in a world of teeth and fur.

CHAPTER 20

In spring, if a bee colony becomes too big or
they run out of space, part of the colony may
leave with the queen to make a new nest.

As we walk back to Henrietta Street after working at the circus, Jonty is almost levitating with joy; he adored working with Albert. He's skipping along the path, babbling on about Miss Primrose and how clever she is.

'Not a word to Papa about any of this, remember, Jonty?' I tell him as we walk up the stairs towards our flat.

'Got it. I'll tell him about Harry and Theo instead.' He mimes locking his mouth and throwing away the key.

I smile. 'Good man.'

I leave Jonty and Papa talking about the Pennefeather boys and I go back down to the workshop. My day hasn't finished yet, not by a long shot.

x x x

At around nine o'clock in the evening I'm standing at the

big white ceramic Belfast sink washing paintbrushes when I hear an almighty crack and then a deep rumbling so loud it seems to roar right through me. I stop dead, feeling very uneasy. What's happening outside? It sounds like a bomb has gone off, but it can't be. Is it thunder?

I let my brushes clatter into the sink and run into the yard. Annie's dashing across the yard's cobblestones towards me, holding her skirts up with one hand.

'Did you hear that noise?' she asks me.

'Yes. And look!' I point at the blast of dust that's pouring into the yard through the archway leading to Henrietta Cottages.

And then we hear loud screaming and shouting.

We look at each other in fright and run through the arch. When we come out the other side what I see is terrifying and I can't take it all in. The air is white with dust and there's a huge pile of rubble at the top of the laneway, at least a storey high. It's cracking and sliding towards the houses at the far side of the laneway, a mess of splintered planks and bricks, like a jagged avalanche.

Dozens of women and men are running away from the rubble, towards us, shouting at the children following them to keep up; many of the women have wailing babies in their arms and everyone looks petrified. Their hair and skin are smothered with dust, their faces bleeding, their clothes torn.

Annie is staring at the rubble. 'Jesus! One of the houses has fallen.'

I look at her in disbelief. That's what the avalanche is? How can a house fall down? But she's right, the house at the top of the laneway, the one nearest the wall to King's Inns, is now a mountain of broken timber and mortar. Every second more bricks and tiles crash down, sending clouds of dust into the air.

And then I notice one small boy standing in front of the rubble, staring at it, a crying toddler in his arms. He's completely frozen.

The horror of what I'm seeing starts to sink in and I feel cold with shock. As we watch, a flood of tiles and then the whole roof slides onto the rubble mountain. People start running out of the other houses on the lane to see what's happening, their extra voices and shouts filling the air.

'Who lives there, Annie?' I ask loudly over the din. 'In the house that's fallen? Where are they?'

She doesn't answer me. Her face is grey and her breath is

starting to get quicker and quicker, her chest rising and falling rapidly. She gives a low moan. 'No! No, no, no!'

Before I know what's happening, she takes off towards the rubble.

'Annie! Come back!' I run after her.

When she reaches the frozen little boy, his face white with brick dust she asks him, 'Peter, where's Joseph?' With his mop of dark hair and green eyes, he's the spit of Joseph McAllister. It must be his little brother. No wonder Annie's so upset.

'He went back in to get Mammy,' the boy says. 'Annie, the roof fell down on top of them. And Raven was in front of the fire. That's not good, is it?'

Ice runs down my spine. The last house on the lane is the McAllisters'. And from what his brother's saying, Joseph's somewhere under all that rubble.

Annie's eyes are wet with tears, but she blinks them away and takes a deep breath. 'Eliza, get Peter and Minnie back from here. It's not safe. And look after them, all right?'

'Where are you going?'

'To find Joseph.'

'You can't, Annie, it's too dangerous,' I say, but she pays no attention. She starts climbing over the rubble, her feet falling through the rocky debris, making her stumble to her knees, but she just gets back up again and again, her legs cut and bleeding.

'Joseph!' she shouts, over and over. 'Joseph, where are you? Joseph?'

I hear the sharp ding-ding-ding of fire engine bells and seconds later firemen jump off the first engine and rush towards us. One of them, an older man who looks like the captain, talks to some of the women and men from the Cottages.

'About seven or eight people unaccounted for,' he shouts at the firemen gathered around him. 'We need to shift that rubble fast and stabilise the house beside it. Don't want it coming down too.'

'Everyone back,' he shouts at the people standing beside the rubble mountain. 'It's not stable. At least ten yards please.'

A fireman puts his hand on my shoulder. 'Miss, you have to move back.'

'But my friend.' I point at Annie who is still clambering over the rubble, shouting for Joseph.

There's another loud crack and tiles from the last part of the roof still attached to the back wall of the house start sliding onto the top of the rubble.

'What's her name?' the fireman asks.

'Annie,' I say.

'Stay here, don't move.' He strides towards her as quickly as he can, calling her name, his black boots sinking into the rubble.

Some people in the crowd start shouting at Annie too.

'Come back, Annie, love. It's too dangerous.'

'Annie? Are you mad, Annie? Turn around!'

Minnie starts to cry and little Peter does his best to soothe her. 'Let's go and see the shiny red fire engine, Minnie,' he says. 'You like fire engines, don't you?'

Minnie nods.

'Good idea, Peter,' I say. 'You take her back there and I'll watch out for Joseph and your mam and make sure Annie's all right.'

He nods at me, but his eyes are sad. He's only around four or five, but I think he knows there isn't much hope for his brother and his mam.

As I watch, the fireman reaches Annie and takes her arm. She shakes it off and moves a few steps away from him. There's another crack and the last slither of roof comes down, one of the wooden beams landing on Annie and the fireman and knocking them to the ground.

'Annie!' I scream, my heart almost coming out of my chest in fright. I'm about to run towards her when another fireman grabs my arm, holding me back.

'Stay here, Miss. You can't help her if you're injured too.'

Three firemen rush to help Annie and their colleague, lifting the timber, helping them out of the debris. Both Annie and the fireman are able to walk, which is a relief, but Annie is lurching and needs to be supported and her left arm is hanging limply by her side. And blood is streaming down the fireman's cheek.

'Annie,' I shout as they pass us. 'Annie.' I will her to look over. I need to see her face, to make sure she's all right, but she doesn't seem to hear me.

A horse-drawn ambulance arrives and Annie is bundled inside and driven away. She'll be all right, I tell myself. She's strong, she'll be all right. I desperately want to go after her, to the hospital, but she asked me to look after Peter and Minnie and that's what I need to do. And Joseph's still under there somewhere. I'm not leaving until he's found.

I move closer to Peter and his little sister. 'Stay beside me now,' I tell Peter.

While one group of firemen put large wooden supports against the house beside the McAllisters, to keep it stable, others start to shift the rubble with shovels, the metal heads hitting off the stones and bricks with loud pings. They lift heavy wooden beams in teams of three or four and dump them away from the rubble. They're doing their best, but it's slow going. It's agony to watch, knowing Joseph is under there. Every second counts.

'Eliza?' I hear a voice and swing around. I've never been so glad to see Jonty in my whole life!

'It *is* you,' he says. 'Papa sent me to find out what's going on and to look for you. We heard fire engines. I almost didn't recognise you with all the dust. I heard someone say Joseph's house fell down, is it true?'

I blink back my tears. I'm far from all right, but I need to keep it together.

'Yes,' I say. 'I'm fine. And it's true, his house is now that pile of rubble.'

My brother's eyes widen. 'A house can do that?'

'I know, it's unbelievable. Jonty, I need you to take Joseph's brother and sister back to our flat. Joseph is under the rubble somewhere and I'm not moving until they pull him out.'

I look at Peter. 'This is my brother, Jonty. He's going to look after you and Minnie. All right?'

Peter nods.

I'm expecting Jonty to put up a fight, to demand to stay and watch the action, but he surprises me.

'I'll get you something to eat,' he tells Peter. 'And Minnie looks tired. She can sleep in my bed.'

Then he turns to me. 'You stay here until they find Joseph, sis. But how will they find him? It's impossible, he could be anywhere.'

That's not exactly true. When the house fell Joseph *was* somewhere – trying to save his mam. I think of something.

'Peter,' I say, 'I need you to concentrate for a moment. Where exactly was your mam this evening? Just before the house fell down.'

'In the kitchen, sewing.'

'How many rooms do you have?'

'Two.'

I look at the house next to the McAllisters' – which is miraculously still standing – and I try to work out the floor plan in my head. I think the two houses were pretty much

193

identical. It's a three-storey building, one room deep, two rooms across, with a narrow hall in the middle, from the look of things.

'Do you go up the stairs to get to your flat?' I ask him.

'Yes,' he says. 'We're on the first floor.'

'Good lad. And is the kitchen on the left or the right of the hall?'

He looks confused.

'From outside, if you are looking at the house. Is your kitchen on this side?' I lift up my right hand. 'Or this side?' I lift up my left.

He closes his eyes for a moment and then opens them again. 'That side.' He points at my left hand. 'And the table is at the window, to get the light. That's where Mam sits.'

'Can you see this street out the window she sits at?' I ask him.

'Yes,' he says. 'I play cowboys with Joe and Mam waves at us through the window.'

'Got it! Well done, Peter.' I rub his head. 'You're a bright lad.'

One of the firemen walks past us carrying a body carefully in his arms, face down. It's a girl about my age. They must have found her in the rubble. Her dress is ripped to shreds and her hair and clothes are matted with dirt and blood. From the way her head is flopped over, it doesn't look good.

I catch Jonty's eye and he gives me a tiny nod.

'Come on, Peter and Minnie,' he says, 'let's leave Eliza to it.'

I'm so grateful for my brother's kindness that I almost cry. But I must stay focused. I scan the mess of bricks and broken wood and try to work out exactly where the kitchen might have been.

Once I'm fairly sure I've located it, I lock my eyes on it and study the area, inch by inch. I'm not sure what I'm expecting to see – a hand rising out of the rubble perhaps – but I can't spot a thing that might be helpful. The air is still thick with dust and it seems to be getting even harder to see. I look at the sky. The light's fading. It must be after half-past nine now.

The hairs on the back of my hands stand up. I know if they don't find Joe and his mam while there's still daylight, they may not make it through the night. I'm terrified, but I have to do this.

The fireman who helped Annie walks past me with a shovel in his hand. There's a bandage wrapped around his head and some blood has seeped through it. I take a deep breath. Come on, Eliza, I tell myself. You can do this.

'Sir,' I say loudly. 'Stop, please!'

He swings around and I can see from the way his eyes soften that he recognises me from earlier. 'It's dangerous up here, Miss. You saw what happened to your friend. Please, stay back.'

'I know where Joseph McAllister and his mother are,' I say, sticking my chin in the air and trying to sound as confident as I can. 'Their brother told me. I want you to dig them out. Joseph is strong and clever and if anyone's alive under there, it's him.'

'Tall Joe McAllister? From the docks?'

I nod. 'Yes.'

'I know Joe. Lovely lad. Where are they, so?'

'I need to come with you. I can't just point. It won't be accurate enough. They probably don't have much time left under there, you need to get it right.'

He looks at me for a moment as if weighing things up and then says, 'All right, Miss. But you're sticking to my side like glue, understand? And if I tell you to get back or move, you do as I say, yes?'

I nod firmly. 'I understand, Sir.'

'Sir?' He gives a laugh. 'Mr Oliver is fine.' He puts his fingers in his mouth and gives an almighty whistle. Several firemen stop what they're doing and rush towards him. He explains what I've just told him. There are a lot of mumblings that I can't quite hear. They don't seem all that keen to take the lead from a girl.

'It's worth trying, lads,' Mr Oliver says. 'She knows the lay-out of the house and where they were when it came down. And she's right about Tall Joe. If anyone can survive this, he can.'

There are more grumbles, but one of the older firemen says, 'Go on then, you lead us, Miss, quick as you can.'

I set off with Mr Oliver close beside me, picking my way over the rubble, the dust getting heavier and heavier until it almost chokes me. There's a strong smell of gas too. It doesn't seem to bother Mr Oliver or the other firemen; they must be used to it. I slip and slice my palm on a sharp piece of brick, but I ignore the sting and the blood and keep going.

When I've reached the top of the heap of rubble, I concentrate hard and stand still on what's left of the collapsed building. I focus on the remaining back wall, stand where the front door would be and then close my eyes, like little Peter did. By the window, he said. I open my eyes, take a few steps to the left, a few steps backwards, then I stop.

'Here,' I say, pointing at the rubble beneath my feet. 'If my hunch is right, they're sheltering under the kitchen table.'

CHAPTER 21

In Greek mythology bees were said to be the messengers of the gods. The ancient Celts believed that bees carried messages from other worlds.

By the time I reach Richmond Hospital the light has completely faded. I still don't know if Joseph and his mother have made it. They were both alive when the firemen dragged them out, but according to Mr Oliver the ambulance men said they were in a bad way and it would be touch and go.

I was right about the kitchen table. The firemen dug through the rubble and found Joseph and his mother both sheltering under it. The table legs had stayed intact, all made from heavy pieces of iron, like the one Joseph had shown me the day he'd rescued Raven. The tabletop was badly cracked, but it had kept the rubble from completely crushing them both.

Mr Oliver explained it had created a shelter over Joe and his mother, shielding them from the falling debris and providing an air pocket for them both to breathe. He also told me which hospital they were taking all the injured to and how to get there. He'd been very kind.

I'm exhausted by the time I get to the entrance of the hospital. The lamps are lit in the entrance gates and there are two horse-drawn ambulances outside. From the dust on the wheels and the horses' legs, I'd say both had been at Henrietta Cottages.

I walk towards the imposing wooden doors, but a security guard in a dark blue uniform stops me.

'I'm here to see Annie O'Hanlon,' I say. 'She was injured at the Henrietta Cottages accident.'

'Are you family?' he asks.

'Not exactly.'

'Direct family only,' he says gruffly.

'But Annie's my tenement family,' I say. 'Doesn't that count?'

The man raises an eyebrow. 'You're from the tenements?'

I nod firmly. 'Yes, Henrietta Street.'

He looks me up and down. 'I don't believe that for one second. You're one of them fancy lady reporters, aren't you? Trying to get a scoop. You're not coming in and that's that.'

I'm too tired to argue. I walk back down the stone steps

and sit on the last one.

'And you can move away from there and all,' he booms down at me. 'No loitering on the steps.'

I sigh wearily and pull myself up. He must feel a bit sorry for me because he adds, 'There's a bench over there.' He points at the patch of lawn to the right of the steps.

'Thanks,' I say. I collapse onto the bench and close my eyes.

X X X

Next thing I know I feel a hand on my shoulder. I open my eyes with a start. I must be seeing things. It can't be. I squeeze them closed and open them again. But no, she's still there, Madam Ada, sitting on the bench beside me, smiling at me gently, Albert by her side. He's not smiling at all. In fact he's positively scowling.

'What were you playing at, 'Liza?' he says. 'You could have got yourself killed, scrambling over the rubble like that.'

'I helped find Joseph, didn't I?'

Madam Ada pats my hand. 'I think you were very brave, *Stellina*. And that's no way to greet a hero, Albert.' She smiles at me again. 'When we heard you were at the hospital, we were worried sick. We thought we'd lost both you and Joseph. We asked some of the neighbours at Henrietta Cottages and they said there were three teenage girls up in the hospital: a girl with a broken arm, a girl who'd climbed over the rubble, risking her own life to save Joseph, and another girl who'd died in the accident. We knew one of them must be you, you see. We were so worried.'

Albert glares at me. 'And you're clearly not dead and you don't have a broken arm so you're the one who could have been killed.'

'As you can see, I'm perfectly fine,' I say a bit huffily. I'm exhausted and he's not being in the least bit helpful. 'And unless you can get me into the hospital, Albert, you can just go away. The security man won't let me in as I'm not family.'

'Eliza!' Madam Ada looks shocked. 'What has got into you both? You're like a pair of wildcats. I'll get you inside. But you need to calm down first.'

'Sorry,' I murmur. But I won't look at Albert, he's too annoying.

Albert stands up. 'I can tell when I'm not wanted.' And with that he strides away, his hands deep in his pockets.

'I'm sorry, Madam Ada, I say. 'It's been a long night and I'm so worried about Joseph and my friend Annie. She's the girl with the broken arm.'

'Forget about Albert, he'll bounce back. Follow me.' She stands up and gives me her hand. 'Say nothing, understand?' She presses her lips together and turns an imaginary key. Just like Albert and Jonty. I smile to myself.

She marches up steps and before the security guard has a chance to utter a word says 'I am Madam Ada Wilde,' sounding just like Mrs Pennefeather. 'I wish to find out information about my employee, Mr Joseph McAllister, who was in that terrible tenement accident. I believe you've already turned my personal assistant, Miss Kane, away. Kindly admit us or your superiors will hear about it first thing in the morning. I have friends in very high places.'

The man gives a small nod. 'I must apologise for that, Ma'am. Thought she were one of those pesky news reporters that have been bothering us. Nurse at the front desk will be able to help you. Sorry about that, Ma'am. Very sorry.'

Madam Ada flounces past him and I follow beside her, my eyes fixed firmly ahead, not looking at him in case I laugh.

'Very high places,' I say in a low voice. 'Especially Lulu and the Fanzinis.'

She gives a laugh. 'Yes. Now there's the desk. Let's hope they know something about Joseph and your friend.'

'Do you have any information about Mr Joseph McAllister?' she asks the nurse at the desk, switching to her normal voice. 'I'm a family friend.'

'He's in surgery, I'm afraid. No news as yet. Awful business. Sorry for your loss. I believe Mrs McAllister was a lovely woman. And leaving those little ones behind, awful.'

Madam Ada reaches forwards, holds onto the edge of the desk and takes a few deep breaths. '*Porco miseria,*' she murmurs. 'My poor Joseph.'

The nurse stands up and rushes around the desk to stand beside Madam Ada. 'Oh my goodness, did you not know? I'm dreadful sorry. Can I get you anything? A glass of water? Tea?'

Madam Ada straightens up. 'That won't be necessary. But there is something else you could help us with.'

x x x

Minutes later I'm sitting beside Annie's hospital bed. The ward nurse has placed a lamp on the small bedside table and it throws a golden light over Annie's face.

'Just five minutes, understand?' the nurse says firmly. 'It's very late and we don't want to disturb the other patients, do we?'

As soon as the nurse starts walking away, the soles of her

shoes squeaking on the wooden floor, Annie asks in a whisper, 'How on earth did you get in here at this hour?'

'Madam Ada. I'll tell you the whole story later, but first I want to hear about your arm. Is it badly broken?'

'No, it was a clean break which is a good thing according to the doctor. This will see it right.' Annie taps her knuckles against the thick white plaster cast covering her arm from wrist to elbow. Her face drops. 'Although I won't be able to work for six weeks. Not sure what we'll do for food.'

'We'll feed you,' I say. 'And I'm sure the other neighbours will want to help too. The tenements stick together, isn't that what you always say?'

She nods. 'True. Any news on Joseph? The nurse told me he's in surgery, but that's all she knew.'

'Nothing else I'm afraid. Jonty is looking after Peter and Minnie. They're sleeping in our flat tonight.'

'Thanks, Eliza. You're the best. And their Mam? Any news there?'

My heart sinks. I don't know how to find the words. I take a deep breath, about to try, but when I look at Annie her eyes are full of tears. I take her hand and hold it tight. 'I'm so sorry,' I say.

'Poor Mrs McAllister. Let's pray Joseph pulls through. Else those poor mites have no one.'

I hear the squeak of the nurse's shoes again. 'I'd better go,' I say.

She gives my hand a squeeze. 'Thanks for everything. I know you helped the firemen find my Joseph. Nurse told me about it – she'd heard from the ambulance drivers who brought him in. When she said it was a small girl with dark hair in plaits who wouldn't take no for an answer I knew exactly who it was. I'll never forget that. You're some friend, Eliza. The best.'

x x x

When I walk outside the hospital, Madam Ada is sitting on the bench waiting for me. She pats the wooden seat beside her.

'How is your friend?' she asks.

'She has a broken arm, but apart from that she's fine, thank goodness. Worried about Joseph, of course. And sad about Mrs McAllister.'

Madam Ada sighs. 'It has been a terrible night. I managed to talk to Joseph's surgeon. He has lost a lot of blood and broken many bones, but they think he'll pull through.'

What a relief! My eyes well up and I blow out my breath and blink the tears away. 'Phew!' I say.

She smiles. 'Phew indeed! Now the poor McAllisters have no mother and no home. They're going to need a lot of support. So I have an idea, *Stellina*. And I'm hoping you can help me. Here's my plan…'

CHAPTER 22

Beekeepers say when a stranger visits one of their
hives the bees will react. As they have such a highly
developed sense of smell, bees may be able to
recognize their keeper by their smell.

The following morning, I stare down at the blank piece of paper, my hand frozen. Draw, Eliza! I tell myself. Start with one line and go from there. But Madam Ada's words keep coming back to me: 'Make it dramatic, eye-catching, bold. We need to attract the biggest crowd possible for the Henrietta Cottages benefit performance. And it all starts with your poster, Eliza.'

The more people who attend, the more money we'll raise for Joseph and his family. That's a lot of pressure! My head is humming with ideas: Madam Ada and her bees. No, Princess Lulu dangling from her teeth; no, Mr Zozimus in his top hat and tails. No, Albert and his dogs. He might be upset if I don't include him. Maybe I should try to include everyone, and all the animals too?

I scrunch up my eyes and try to calm my mind. 'Concentrate, Eliza,' I tell myself. 'You can do this.' I hear a buzzing and I open my eyes. A worker bee has flown in the open workshop window and is perching on my desk. I stare at her for a moment, taking deep breaths and watching her as she rests.

I *can* do this – I do it every week for different clients. This month alone I've drawn and painted Celtic symbols and exotic animals like elephants and giraffes. I need to treat the circus like my newest and most important client.

And then it comes to me. I know exactly what to put in the middle of the poster. I pull out my sketchbook, find the right pages and study them. My drawing hand springs to life and within seconds I'm lost in a riot of pencil lines.

X X X

As arranged, Madam Ada arrives at midday on the button to collect my poster design and deliver it to the printers. The benefit is next Saturday, 17 June, exactly one week away, so we don't have much time to spread the news. The printers have kindly promised to work all afternoon, evening and tomorrow (even though it's a Sunday) to get it ready for the poster boys. They're printing leaflets too, all free of charge.

The poster boys will put it up on lampposts and billboards all over Dublin city and all the messenger boys on Henrietta Street and around the area have promised to put a leaflet through every letter box in town. Everyone's being so kind!

I hear a knock on the workshop door, put down my ink pen and step away from my desk. I'd love more time to work on the poster, but it will have to do.

I pull open the door. I half expected to see Albert with her, but Madam Ada is alone. I try to cover my disappointment but, yet again, she catches me out.

'Albert sends his regards,' she says with a smile. 'He wanted to come today, but we have much to do to get ready for next weekend. I've added a special free show on Saturday morning for the tenement families from Henrietta Cottages and Henrietta Street. They have been through a lot in the last few days and helped the McAllister family so much. It's our way of showing support.'

'As well as the benefit performance?'

She nods. 'Yes. The price of a ticket for the benefit is too expensive for most families I'm sure. Speaking of the benefit, I have a favour to ask, Eliza.'

She pushes a strand of my hair back off my face, her fingers warm against my cool skin. When I'm drawing I often get very cold as my body's still for hours, apart from my drawing hand.

'I'd like you to say a few words at the benefit performance,' she says.

I look at her, thinking she's joking, but she looks perfectly serious. 'Me? Why me?'

'You live here and you saw what happened first-hand. And you know Joseph and his family.'

'I've only just moved here. What about Joseph himself, he'd be great?'

'I don't think Joseph will be well enough by next Saturday. Eliza, you are an observer. You watch the world carefully. I have seen the attention you give your drawing. I believe you will find the right words to say, and I believe you have the strength and the passion to deliver them.'

'How about you?' I suggest. 'Or Mr Zozimus or Albert or my friend Annie?'

She smiles gently. 'Anyone but you, is that what you are saying?'

I nod, my face going red. 'I'd be too nervous. I'm sorry. I

just can't.'

'Think about it.' She takes my hand and gives it a squeeze. 'Write the speech. And if you truly cannot deliver it on the day, I will. Do we have a deal?'

'Yes.' I feel a rush of relief, but also a strange flatness. I don't have long to worry about it because then Madam Ada says, 'So the poster. Is it ready?'

I lead her towards the desk. 'I hope you like it.' I'm always nervous about a client's reaction, but with this client even more so.

She sighs and my heart drops. But then she says, 'I love it! Dramatic, mysterious, other. Putting Rex and Karina in the middle is genius, and that border with all the entwined animals and the beautiful lettering.' She puts her fingers to her mouth and kisses them. '*Bellissimo*. How did you create such beauty in one morning?'

'I got up early,' I say, proud as punch that she likes it. 'I was in the workshop at sunrise.'

'How can I ever thank you, *Stellina*?' She throws her arms around me and gives me a surprisingly strong hug. Mama gave the most fantastically strong hugs too and for a second I pretend its Mama holding me.

Madam Ada draws back. 'Such talent! But now, I must get this work of art to the printers. Would you like to come with me?'

'I'd love to but I have to catch up on work this afternoon and then I need to prepare dinner for everyone and visit Annie in hospital. And Joseph if they'll let me.'

'Of course. Are Joseph's siblings still with you?'

'Yes. Jonty's playing with them outside. He's been really good with them.'

She reaches into her pocket and draws out a small black velvet purse. 'Will you give your brother this from me? Tell him I'll be very disappointed if he doesn't spend it all on sweets for himself and the *bambini*.' She hands me a shiny new penny.

'Thank you, he'll be over the moon,' I say. 'I'll see you on Monday, Madam Ada. Break a leg this at this evening's performance.'

'Thank you, *Stellina*.'

I can't hold my curiosity in anymore.

'Madam Ada, what does that mean? *Stellina*? I know "*Stella*" means star, but the "*-lina*" part?'

She smiles, but there's a strange sadness behind her eyes.

'Little Star. Now, the circus awaits. *Ciao, Stellina.*' She kisses her fingers and blows them at me.

Little star? It's a lovely thing to call me, but somehow I feel there's more to the name than she's letting on.

x x x

At five that evening I feed Jonty, Peter and Minnie bowls of bacon, cabbage and potato stew as a special treat. Peter eats everything on his plate, quickly, as if it might be taken away from him if he pauses. Minnie eats only a little of the potato and drinks a few sips of milk. I think she's pining for her mam.

Papa is resting in his room. He'll eat later. I think he's finding the noise difficult. Minnie is very sweet, but she is only two. She doesn't usually say much, but when she does open her mouth, oh boy! She woke up at five in the morning and cried for her mam for over an hour, until Peter managed to settle her down. Papa said they can stay as long as they need to, but it's not ideal. Jonty is back at school tomorrow and I need to work. I'm hoping Annie will have a plan.

'Would you like more stew, Peter?' I ask him.

His eyes widen. 'There's more?'

'Yes, you can finish it.' I ladle another spoonful into his

bowl and he tucks in immediately. I'm giving him my help-ing, but I can fill up on bread.

'And after dinner Jonty will take you to the shops to buy you each a treat,' I say. 'All thanks to Madam Ada. What's your favourite, Peter? Do you like chocolate or marshmal-lows or toffee?'

Peter's mouth falls open. Luckily he's swallowed all his food. 'Don't know,' he says. 'Never had any of 'em.'

'Chocolate then,' Jonty says firmly. 'You'll love it, Peter. Minnie too. Then we'll play cowboys outside until it's bed-time. How does that sound?'

'Magic,' Peter says, sounding just like Jonty. 'Is our house fixed yet? Can we sleep there? Will Mam be coming for us soon? Or Joseph?'

Jonty looks at me. We haven't told them about their mam yet. Papa thought it was best to wait and let Joseph break the sad news.

'You'll be staying here tonight,' I say, leaving it at that.

'Magic,' Peter says again. 'Can we go to the shops now, Jonty?'

''Ops,' Minnie says. 'Go 'ops, 'onty.' She puts her little arms out for Jonty to pick her up. She loves being carried by Jonty.

We all laugh.

'I'll see you later, sis,' Jonty says. 'Come here, Princess Minnie.' He picks her up and rests her on his hip. 'Wave bye-bye to Eliza.'

As I walk towards Richmond Hospital I smile to myself. Who knew Jonty would make such an excellent nursemaid? But Peter asked an important question. Where *are* they going to live?

x x x

Luckily, Annie does have a plan. In fact she makes the hospital release her early so we walk back to Henrietta Street together.

'Would you like to take my arm?' I ask her at the top of the hospital steps. She stops dead and stares at me.

'Have you gone stark raving mad, Eliza Kane? I'm no invalid. I have a broken arm, that's all. Left one too, thank the Lord. I'll be back to work as soon as the McAllister nippers are sorted, cast or no cast.'

'But the doctor said you need to rest.'

She gives a snort. 'Rest? We need the money. I'll rest when I'm dead.' Her face drops for a moment. 'Sorry, I shouldn't have said that. Not right to joke about being dead, not with poor Joseph's mam and all.'

'How is Joseph today?' I ask her. 'Any news?'

'Concussion. Crushed ribs, broken leg and arm, lots of cuts and bruises. He won't be out of hospital for a while. But he'll live, that's the main thing. Not like his poor mam.'

She goes quiet for a moment. 'Eliza, it's so awful. Those poor little ones.' She stops and presses both hands over her mouth. Tears fall down her face. 'Sorry, I think it's just starting to sink in.'

'You're probably still in shock,' I say. 'Do you want to sit down for a second?'

She nods and I lead her towards the bench I shared with Madam Ada and Albert. It seems like a lifetime ago but it was only last night.

When we're sitting, she puts her head down and takes a couple of deep breaths. 'Sorry, didn't mean to get so upset there.'

'Stop saying sorry,' I tell her. 'It's hard being strong all the time, Annie. You're allowed to cry every now and then.'

Tears flow down her face and this time she doesn't apologise for them. 'It is hard.' She blows out her breath in a whoosh and wipes away her tears with her fingers. After a few moments she says, 'How are Peter and Minnie today?'

'They're doing well. Asking for their mam.'

'They don't know yet?'

'Papa thought it best they hear it from Joseph.'

She nods. 'That is best all right. They should be able to visit him tomorrow, all being well.'

'Papa says they can stay with us for the moment. And Jonty's being brilliant. Minnie adores him and he's carrying her around like a new puppy.'

Annie laughs. 'I can't wait to see that. Don't worry, once I've talked to Da and the boys I'll take them both in until Joseph's better. They feel bad about my arm so I'm sure they'll say yes. You'll only need to have them one more night.'

'Annie, are you sure? There are already seven of you in your flat.'

She shrugs. 'Two more won't make any difference. I'm sure one of the neighbours will take Minnie in when I'm cleaning. And George can keep an eye on Peter and take him to school and back. Mrs McAllister made him go every day, it's... it was ... important to her that he can read and write.'

She stands up. 'Now, let's get home.' We start walking down the driveway towards the gates.

'And I want to hear all about this circus benefit performance,' she says. 'One of the nurses told me about it. Her husband works at *The Freeman's Journal*. It's big news apparently. Some famous Irish opera singer has agreed to sing an aria from *Madam Butterfly*, whatever that is. During the circus I mean.'

'Oh,' I say, feeling a bit flattened. Madam Ada didn't say anything about an opera singer. Maybe they won't use my poster now. They'll get a proper artist to do one, with a picture of the singer.

'What is it, Eliza? You've gone very quiet.'

'Nothing.' It seems wrong to worry about my artwork when Annie's just out of hospital and the McAllisters have lost their mam and their home. 'I hope the benefit raises a heap of money for Joseph's family and the others.'

She links my arm with her good right arm. 'Me too.'

Then I remember something. 'Annie, would you give a speech at the benefit? About the McAllisters and everything they've been through and how they need our support. I can help you write it if you like.'

She laughs. 'Me? Give a speech? I'd rather have my teeth pulled out with a rusty pliers. No thank you. You should do it, Eliza. You're good with words.'

'That's what Madam Ada said,' I say glumly. 'But I'd rather not.'

'Don't be such a scaredy cat.'

'What if I mess it up?'

'Then you mess it up. No one will mind. They'll all be there to show support for the families, they probably won't even notice if you stumble over your words a bit.' She stops dead in her tracks and stares at the lamp post in front of us. 'Blimey, that's good. The lion looks so real.'

It's one of my circus posters. An extra strip of paper has been pasted across the bottom saying 'Just added to the bill – the Irish Nightingale, Miss Catherine Bright'. So they did use my poster after all. It *is* good enough.

'Meet the artist,' I say, my heart full.

'Never!' Annie says. 'Eliza, I'm so proud of you. And you know what would make me even prouder? She nudges me with her shoulder. 'Hearing you give a speech about the McAllisters at the circus benefit. Will you do it?'

CHAPTER 23

Honeybees do not hibernate. In the winter, when it is
too cold to fly, they cluster tightly together in their
hive to stay warm.

By the Saturday of the benefit I'm a bundle of nerves. The circus performers and animals have been working hard all week, giving shows every day and practising new acts for the benefit.

Albert and Jonty have been training Miss Primrose to box. Luca helped Albert make a small wooden boxing ring with ropes and a floor painted red with a gold star in the middle.

I had to muck out the ring by myself every day as Albert was so busy with his dogs. But it meant I got to see the Flying Fanzinis' new act and boy, is it good! And I got to meet Karina's huge ten-foot python, Tiny, up close and personal. Karina let me stroke his skin. I was expecting it to be slimy, but it was cool, smooth and dry, a bit like rubbing leather.

I've been working hard too – painting in the workshop, cooking and cleaning at home, helping at the circus from five to seven every day, and minding Minnie in the evenings so Annie can visit Joseph in hospital. Jonty and George have been keeping an eye on Peter together. They've become quite the little gang, the three of them.

I barely had time to breathe all week, let alone write a speech for the benefit. I was up until one in the morning last night trying to think of the right words.

It's six in the morning now. I woke up at five and couldn't get back to sleep. It must be all the excitement of today's show. I sit up in bed. My notebook is on my bedside table and I pick it up.

'My name is Eliza Kane,' I write in it. 'And I'm, I'm…' I'm what? It doesn't matter who I am.

'Agghh!' I tear out the page and throw it on the floor.

All I really want to say is 'Please give Joe and the families money. They are in trouble and they need your help.' But I know I need to say more, to tell their story properly. Think, Eliza, think!

Then I hear Mama's voice in my head. I had to write an essay once for school about why all girls should get the chance to go to college and I remember her telling me: 'Start at the beginning, Eliza and be honest on the page, tell your truth.' She said that a lot: 'Tell your truth.'

I try again on a fresh page. 'My name is Eliza Kane,' I write. 'And I want to tell you about what happened last week at Henrietta Cottages...'

I sigh. It's not perfect, but it's a start. I keep writing.

x x x

Over breakfast I take a big gamble. I have to explain where we'll be all afternoon and I've decided to tell Papa the truth, kind of.

While spooning out the porridge I say, 'Papa, Annie has two spare tickets for the circus benefit performance this afternoon at two o'clock. Can I bring Jonty? He's been so good with Peter and Minnie all week and Annie thought it would be a nice treat for him.'

'Can we go, Papa, please?' Jonty says. 'That would be magic!' I told Jonty about my plan earlier this morning and he plays along beautifully.

While Papa thinks for a moment my heart almost stops. What if he says no?

But to my great relief he says, 'I went to the circus with

your mother once. Quite the experience. That's really kind of Annie. Tell her I said thank you.'

Phew! Jonty grins at me and I grin back. Circus here we come!

x x x

Jonty sings and does funny little jigs the whole way down the stairs, out the door and along Dorset Street until we reach the circus tent. 'Da-da, diddely, da-da-da-da, circus Jonty, circus 'Liza, circus, circus, circus!'

Jonty and I are going a bit early to help out. We're meeting Annie, Minnie and Peter there. Madam Ada has given us ringside seats together.

As we reach the tent, the main entrance flap is closed and secured from the inside. From the music playing, a surging and sweeping waltz, the Flying Fanzinis are practising their new trapeze act.

'What do we do now?' Jonty asks.

'We go around the back,' I say. 'What Albert calls the back door.'

'Like real circus performers?'

I smile. 'Like real circus performers.'

As soon as we walk into the smaller tent, Albert gives us a

huge smile. 'There's my favourite Dubliners. All set for your speech, 'Liza?'

I pat the pocket of my skirt and feel my sketchbook safely inside. I feel a tingle of nerves race up my spine and right to the tips of my fingers. I nod. 'I hope so.'

'Good girl yourself. Now Aunt Ada has a job for you both.' He points at the open cardboard box which is sitting on top of Coco's equipment chest.

I peer inside the box and see – my lion drawing! Printed in black ink on white card with a fancy gold border. 'What is that?' I ask.

'A programme, like in a theatre. The names of all the acts are inside. Fancy, eh? Aunt Ada got them printed especially for today's show.' He takes one out and hands it to Jonty. 'Your sister's one heck of an artist. Once we open the doors your job is to welcome people and to hand out the programmes. If you're up for it.'

x x x

We definitely are up for it, especially Jonty who throws himself into the job.

'Welcome to the greatest show on earth,' he tells the first family who walk inside the tent, a big grin on his face. 'Here's your programme, enjoy the show.'

I'm so nervous about my speech that I'm finding it hard to smile. My hands have started to tremble and I feel sick. I can't do it, I just can't.

'Jonty, will you be all right on your own for a few minutes?' I say in a rush. 'I need to find Madam Ada.'

'Sure thing, sis,' he says, without taking his eyes off the next family coming in and thrusting a programme into the mother's hands. 'Welcome, you lucky, lucky people. Boy, have you got a treat in store. Lions, snakes, boxing dogs…' He's in his element.

The door of Madam Ada's golden caravan is closed so I knock on it, hoping there's no one with her.

'Who is it?' she says from inside.

'Eliza,' I say.

'*Stellina*, come in, come in!'

I step inside, relieved to see she is indeed alone. She's sitting at her dressing table. On it is a large silver backed hairbrush, like the one Mama used to have. She's pinned her hair on top of her head and threaded white feathers and ribbon through it. It looks magical.

'What do you think?' she asks me, moving her head from

side to side.

'*Bellissimo*,' I say, using one of her favourite Italian words.

She smiles. 'Ready for your speech?'

'That's why I'm here,' I say. 'I don't think I can do it. My stomach feels like it's full of bees and my hands are shaking, look!' I stick out my right hand.

'All performers have nerves,' she says. 'It means you care deeply about the show. It is a good thing. No nerves, no passion.' She stands up and points at the dressing-table stool. 'Sit,' she says, reminding me of how Albert talks to his dogs.

I do as she says. She takes the ribbons from the end of my plaits and before I have a chance to say anything, picks up her hairbrush and starts brushing out my hair. She starts to French plait it, her hands moving like a flash. '*Stellina*, you need to face your fears. You may find out that, like Rex, they are largely toothless.'

'But what if I make a mess of the speech?'

She shrugs. 'It does not matter. What matters is that you tried. Admit to the audience that you are nervous. They will understand. This speech, it is not about you, it is about the McAllisters. Tell everyone what happened and what you saw in your own words. Tell your truth.'

With a start I realise what she just said: 'Tell your truth'. Like Mama!

As her fingers move through my hair my mind whirls. Is she right? If I make a mess will people forgive me? Annie said that too. Maybe they're both right.

When she's finished plaiting my hair she says *'Perfetto.'*

I look in the mirror. I see a new Eliza Kane, older and more sophisticated. Or so I try to tell myself.

But am I brave enough to do this, to tell my truth?

x x x

As the Fanzinis whip across the tent on their flying trapezes, swinging high in the air and catching each other by their hands and the feet, I try not to think about my upcoming speech, but it's hard. My stomach feels like I'm up there with Fanzinis, whirling, swooping and flipping.

Even Karina and Tiny can't keep my mind off it. Minnie isn't keen on the snakes. She squeals and puts her hands over her eyes until they've gone. Annie gives her a cuddle.

'Don't be scared, Minnie,' Jonty says. 'Albert's dogs are up next.'

He's right: as soon as Karina and her snakes are out of the ring, Albert runs through the velvet curtains with Miss

Primrose. She's wearing tiny boxing gloves on her front paws.

Jonty is already in fits of giggles and the act hasn't even started yet. 'This is going to be so good,' he says.

The music gets faster and faster as Albert lifts Miss Primrose into the ring. She jumps onto her hind legs and starts moving her front paws, just like she's boxing. Albert pretends to box her and after a few rounds, Miss Primrose wins. I smile despite my swirling stomach.

Next up is Karina and her lions and this time Minnie watches through her fingers. I'm so distracted by my nerves it feels like I'm watching the acts through a sheet of glass.

'When's your speech?' Annie asks me as the lions' cage is cleared away and Coco takes to the ring to make everyone laugh.

'Just before the finale,' I tell her. 'I have to go and get ready when the opera singer starts.'

'Good luck,' she says, squeezing my hand. 'I'll be the one whooping at the end. I'm so proud of you, Eliza. You're really brave.'

'I don't feel brave, I feel terrified.'

'And that's what makes you so brave. Feeling scared and doing it anyway.'

'Thanks, Annie.'

X X X

I listen to Miss Bright from the small tent, her voice soaring up, up, up into the tippy top of the circus tent, like the Fanzinis, and then down again. Like my stomach feels right now in fact, like I'm on one of those roller coasters!

Then I hear a second voice, joining Miss Bright's, the two voices blending perfectly, as bright and delicate as shards of light, like two butterflies dancing together in the air.

Albert is sitting on a closed trunk, his head in his hands, listening. I look over at him.

'Is that Madam Ada singing with Miss Bright?' I ask him in a low voice, not wanting to spoil the atmosphere.

'Yes,' he says. 'Isn't it beautiful?'

I nod. '*Bellissimo.*'

He pats the trunk. I sit down beside him and we listen together, in spellbound silence. For a moment I almost forget my anxiety. When they finish the tent goes utterly quiet for a moment before nearly exploding with applause.

'I guess they like it then,' Albert says. 'Ready, 'Liza? Let's walk out together.' He stands up and holds out his hand.

CHAPTER 24

*When a queen retires, the colony feeds a few chosen female
larvae with royal jelly. The first young bee to break out of
her cell usually becomes the new queen. Sometimes a
young queen bee has to fight the other young queen
bees to win her title.*

Standing in the ring when it's full of people is a very
different experience to mucking it out when the tent is
empty. I look around at all the expectant faces, girls and boys
in their Sunday best, ladies in fancy hats, gentlemen in smart
three-piece suits. Not the usual circus audience at all. Far
more well-to-do.

I'm standing on the small stage in the middle of the ring,
with Madam Ada right beside me. 'I'm here in case you need
me,' she says in a low voice. 'But you can do this, *Stellina*.'

I give her a nod and as much of a smile as I can manage.

Mr Zozimus' voice rings out from in front of the stage.
'And now, ladies and gentlemen, boys and girls, Miss Eliza

Kane would like to say a few words about tonight's benefit performance.' He looks up at me. That's my cue to start. I hold my sketchbook firmly in my hand, open at the page where the speech starts. I'm going to try and speak without it, but it's there just in case, like the Fanzinis' safety net.

I take a deep breath and begin. 'Thank you for coming tonight. As Mr Wilde said I'm Eliza, Eliza Kane.' My voice falters so I stop and take another deep breath.

'I'm sorry, I'm very nervous, but I'm going to do my best to tell you what happened last week at Henrietta Cottages. A member of this circus, Joseph McAllister, tragically lost his mother and also his home. He and his siblings and the other families from Henrietta Cottages deserve our support.' It comes out in a bit of a rush but I don't falter and I'm talking as loudly as I can, so everyone can hear.

'I live on Henrietta Street. We have a workshop in the yard and I was working there on Friday evening when I heard a terrible noise outside, cracking and rumbling. I thought it was thunder at first, it was so loud. I ran out to see what was happening and found my friend, Annie O'Hanlon, in the yard. There were screams and shouts and we ran out to Henrietta Cottages.

'What we found out there was horrible. Really horrible. It was like a bomb had gone off in one of the houses, there was nothing left but rubble. And the dust. It almost made me choke. And the bodies being carried out. It was so awful I couldn't take it all in.' I gulp, swallowing back tears.

'Anyway, Annie bravely ran across the rubble to try and find her friend Joseph McAllister. Some of you might know him as Tall Joe. A floor timber fell on her and she broke her arm. She's all right, thank goodness. She's looking after Peter and Minnie McAllister while Joseph recovers in hospital. They're little, only five and two.

'As you all know I'm sure, six people lost their lives when number one Henrietta Cottages collapsed. I'd like to read out their names:

'Mrs Jean McAllister, Joseph, Minnie and Peter's mother; Elizabeth Sommers, who was only four, and her brother, Eugene Sommers who lost his life trying to save her, a real hero; Jane Rose and her brother Patrick, who was only three, and their aunt, Mrs Fahy.

Let's have a moment of silence for all those lost souls.'

The tent goes deathly quiet for what seems like forever. I count to ten in my head then continue.

'I've only just started working for this circus, but Joseph McAllister has worked with the Wildes and all their circus family for four years. All the funds from this evening's performance will go towards supporting him and Minnie and Peter, and the others.

'Everyone has been really kind already. But Joseph took a real battering – he was lucky to survive and he'll be in hospital for weeks – and he won't be able to work for months. All they want is to stay together. They don't need much, just a roof over their heads and something to eat.

'We are hoping tonight's benefit will raise enough to pay their rent until Joseph can get back to work and support his family.

'I haven't lived on Henrietta Street for very long, but there is one thing I know for sure. The people who live here and at Henrietta Cottages have such big hearts. They have been nothing but kind to me and my brother. And family means everything to the people who live in the tenements. It means safely, it means loyalty, it means love.

'So thank you for coming to this special benefit performance. You have already made a real difference to the families by being here.

'Joseph asked me to pass on his thanks to you all. And to the firemen who pulled him out. I know some of you are here this evening.'

There's a hearty cheer from the seats to the right of me and everyone laughs.

'Three cheers for our brave Dublin firemen,' a lady shouts. 'Hip hip hooray! Hip hip hooray! Hip hip hooray!'

When the cheering and applause die down I say 'And a final thank you to Madam Ada Wilde. This benefit was her idea and thank you to all the circus family for taking part today, and to Miss Catherine Bright. And now, on with the show!'

'Well said, young lady,' a gentleman shouts.

Everyone starts clapping again and lots of people jump to their feet including Jonty and Annie, who cheer wildly. A standing ovation! I spot Albert standing beside them, cheering the loudest of all.

CHAPTER 25

A honeybee's abdomen or stomach holds a stinger and a sack of venom. Its stripes warn other animals to keep away, that it has a painful sting.

'Thirty-four bloomin' pounds! Are you serious, Eliza? That's more than a shop girl earns in a whole year.' Annie grins at me and practically dances in the yard. She was outside finishing up the washing when I found her. 'Wait till my Joseph hears. He'll be over the moon, so he will.'

'*My* Joseph?' I say with a grin.

'Stop teasing me! The accident made me realise, well, you know.'

'How much you like him?'

She smiles. 'Something like that. When did you find out? About the money I mean?'

'Madam Ada told me the news today when I was working at the circus. Took them two days to count all the extra coins in the buckets.' We'd placed buckets at the exit for people to throw any loose change into.

'Can I tell Joseph the good news when I visit him tonight, Eliza? Or would Madam Ada like to tell him herself?'

'No, she's happy for you to do it. She said she'd visit him tomorrow morning. She'd like to help him find somewhere clean and safe for the family to live and organise the first few month's rent.'

'They'll all get more than a few month's rent for that kind of money,' Annie says. 'Three cheers for Madam Ada.' She grabs both my hands and dances me around the yard.

x x x

Still a little breathless from all the dancing, I collect Jonty from outside the workshop where he's waiting for me after studying late at the Pennefeathers and we go upstairs to Papa together.

'Can I come to the circus with you tomorrow after school?' he asks. 'And every day from now until they go. Please, Eliza? I'm fed up with all the studying with Theo and Harry.'

'Maybe. I'll talk to Mr Stephens.'

'Thanks, sis.'

I know the circus will be leaving Dublin at the end of the month so Jonty's right, we need to pack in as much time there as we possibly can. I'm not thinking about what happens after they're gone. It's too sad to imagine.

We reach the top of the stairs and I push open the door to our flat. Papa is sitting at the dining table, staring at the doorway. It looks like he's been waiting for us. As we walk inside he learns towards us, his eyes peering hard, trying to focus on our faces.

'Where have you been?' he says, his voice low and intense. 'I want the truth now, Eliza.'

'It's Tuesday,' I say. 'I was collecting Jonty from the Pennefeathers. Are we late, Papa?'

'I did not bring you up to lie to me, Eliza. Where were you this afternoon? Where have you been every afternoon recently? I want to know the truth.'

All the blood drains from my face and I feel sick. He knows about the circus! How?

'Papa,' I say. 'It's not what you think. I'm still drawing every afternoon.'

'Mr Pennefeather is the liar, is that it? He took me for a surprise lunch today and told me all about your speech. He was at the benefit on Saturday, Eliza. He clearly heard you say you've been working at the circus. Is that why it's taking you so long to do every piece of illumination?'

'I work really hard on the illuminations,' I say, my pulse racing and my face flaring red, not that Papa can see it. I have to try and explain why I've been lying to him. 'I get up early to do them and I work late too. But yes, I've also been working at the circus, trying to earn some extra money. I didn't think I'd like the circus work. It's mostly mucking out horse dung, but I've got used to it. The circus people are kind, Papa. They raised a huge amount of money for the McAllisters.'

Papa shakes his head. 'The circus is a dangerous place. So dangerous. What if something happened to you? A terrible accident. You could be kicked by a horse, a crocodile could bite you. Or you could be mauled by a lion.'

'They don't have crocodiles, Papa,' Jonty puts in. 'Only snakes. And Rex didn't maul me. I took my arm out before-'

'Jonty!' I snap. He stops immediately, realising what he's just said.

There's an icy silence in the room.

Finally Papa says 'So you have Jonty tied up in this too, Eliza? Is he studying at the Pennefeathers' at all after school or was that also a lie?'

'He is, Papa. On a Tuesday and a Thursday.'

240

Papa shakes his head. 'After all they've done for this family you deceive them too? Oh, Eliza. Why didn't you ask me about working at the circus?'

'Because you would have said no,' I say, balling up my hands. 'You don't care about what I want to do. You made me leave college so I could be your servant. Cooking, cleaning, and looking after you and Jonty. What *I* want doesn't matter at all. I'm only a stupid girl.' I can hear my voice getting louder and louder, but I don't care. 'I'm exhausted keeping this family together,' I continue. 'I tried to do something good, to pay for the eye operation you won't even talk about. I did it for Jonty too. You should see him working with the dogs, it makes him so happy. I am sorry about lying to you, Papa. But I'm not sorry about working at the circus.'

'Stop shouting at me, Eliza!' Papa says. 'I've never heard such rudeness. You will go to the circus tomorrow after work – your proper work – and tell them you won't be back. You are never, ever to go near the circus again after that, do you understand me? That goes for you too, Jonty. From now on the circus is banned.'

'No, Papa!' Jonty says. 'Please let us work there. They'll be leaving soon and we'll work extra hard after that. I won't go to the Pennefeathers if I can't work at the circus.'

Papa turns to me. 'See, Eliza! Now your brother thinks he can be insolent and rude also. Enough! Go to your room and stay there.'

'But Papa-' I say.

'Not one more word, Eliza, I'm warning you. Your poor departed mother would be so disappointed in you. Go!'

I stare at him. What a horrible thing to say about Mama. I run into our room, throw myself down on my bed and bury my head in my pillow. Hot angry tears soak into the pillowcase. No circus? I can't bear it. Why did Mr Pennefeather have to tell Papa about my speech? I know it's not his fault: he wasn't to know it was a secret, but it's ruined everything.

X X X

The following morning Papa barely says a word to us over breakfast.

'You know what you have to do later, Eliza?' he says as I leave for the workshop.

'Yes, Papa,' I say glumly.

'Once that is done the word circus is banned from this house, do you hear me, both of you?'

'Yes, Papa,' we say. Jonty's eyes are red and his face is pale.

He looks like he's barely slept.

As we walk down the stairs together Jonty says, 'Eliza, will you say goodbye to Albert for me? And all the dogs? To everyone. Tell them they're all magic.'

'Of course I will. I'm so sorry about all this, Jonty.'

'It's not your fault.' He looks at me, his eyes blurry with tears. 'I'll just miss them all so much.'

'I know, me too.'

He goes quiet then and we walk in silence. What is there to say? Our magical time with the circus is over. Our hearts are broken.

x x x

I try to concentrate on designing Mr Pennefeather's decorated poem, but it's hard as he's the one who told Papa. And knowing I have to face Madam Ada later and admit I lied to her too, the very thought of it makes my stomach twist.

Mr Pennefeather's favourite poem is by an Irish writer called W.B. Yeats. I decide to write out the text first. I can add in a border later, when I feel less sad and angry. Right now, plain black lettering is about all I can manage.

I found the poem in one of Mama's books. I read it and start to cry. It's all about treading on someone's dreams.

I have spread my dreams under your feet, it says. *Tread softly because you tread on my dreams.*

My own dreams have been completely crushed. Like a 'clock', a disgusting tenement cockroach, under a boot. Squashed dead.

X X X

As I walk towards the circus compound at five o'clock that evening my heart is so heavy it feels like a rock in my chest. My mouth is dry and I swallow, trying to get rid of the lump in my throat.

I have no idea what Madam Ada is going to say to me, but I'm dreading it. Whatever about disappointing Papa, disappointing Madam Ada is just as bad.

'Hey, 'Liza,' Albert calls. He's sitting on the steps of his caravan, repairing one of the dogs' costumes, a sewing needle in his hand. 'You all right?'

'Albert, I have to talk to Madam Ada. She'll explain everything. Jonty said to say goodbye. And that he'll miss you and the dogs. And all the circus family. He said to say you're all magic.'

'Goodbye? Are you moving away, 'Liza?'

I know if I get into it I'll start to cry. 'Something like that,'

I say. 'Thanks for everything, Albert. I have to go now.' I walk quickly towards Madam Ada's caravan.

A moment later I hear him running after me. "Liza, wait! I have something for you.' He hands me a tiny wooden dog, no bigger than my thumb. I look at it carefully. It's Pepper.

'Something to remember me by,' he says. 'Carved it myself.'

'It's beautiful, thank you. I'm sorry, I don't have anything for you.'

He gives me a wink. 'Come back and find me next year. Same time, same place. Better than a present. I don't know what's going on, 'Liza and I can see you don't want to talk about it. But find me, please. I'll be here waiting for you. The thought of seeing you again next year, that will keep me going through the winter. I've never had a friend like you before.'

I nod, biting the inside of my cheek to try and stop myself crying. Maybe Papa will have cooled down by next summer. There's always hope.

'I will, I promise,' I say.

He nods. We stand there for a long moment, staring at each other. He gives me a gentle smile. 'Not easy saying goodbye to a friend is it? You're magic, 'Liza.'

I give a laugh. 'You know it's Jonty's new favourite word now, thanks to you? Bye, Albert. You're magic too.'

With one last nod he turns and slowly walks back to his caravan.

I knock on the door of the golden caravan for one last time. 'Madam Ada?'

'Enter, *Stellina*. I've been expecting you.'

I step into the caravan and she waves at the sofa. She doesn't look cross, her eyes are kind and I feel so relieved. I sit down and she settles herself beside me. Orange blossom and honey. I breathe it in, trying to hold on to the scent.

'I've had a message from your father – he asked a messenger boy to come and tell me – apologising for your behaviour. He says this will be your last visit. It seems he did not know you were working here.'

I can feel my cheeks burn. 'I'm so sorry,' I say. 'I should never have lied to you. Jonty just wanted to work here so much. And after the first day I started to love it too.' I look down at my hands, feeling hollow and horribly embarrassed.

She lifts my chin with her finger. 'I knew you did not have

his permission.'

I stare at her in surprise. 'But you let us work for you anyway. Why?'

'You needed us,' she says simply. 'I recognise a broken heart when I see one. My heart was once broken too.'

As I watch her face softens. 'I had a daughter called Stella. She got very sick, like your mama. Died when she was only three.'

'Oh, Madam Ada, I'm so sorry. That's so sad.'

'It is sad, very sad. She was *il mio cuore*, my heart. And she is always here,' she places her hand over her heart. 'As your mama is in your heart.

'Your papa is angry right now, but his anger will soften. I do not apologise for taking you and Jonty into our circus family. It was the right thing to do. And in time maybe your papa will see that. Maybe not. Either way, it has been a joy, *Stellina*. Be brave and follow your own path, even if it is a difficult one. I expect great things of you. And I know your Mama does also.'

'Papa said she'd be disappointed in me. For lying and for working here.'

She tilts her head. 'And what do *you* think? Is he right?'

It hadn't occurred to me to question what he said. I think about this carefully. I think about Mama. She was passionate about lots of things: making sure girls got a chance to go to school, teaching French, singing, dancing, gardening, nature, science, bees ... so many things. And me. I know she loved me with all her heart. She told me over and over again, even before she got sick.

'No,' I say. 'I think he was wrong. I should never have lied to him or to you, that wasn't right. But I think she would have loved your circus. And you, Madam Ada.'

And then something else comes to me: I've kept our family alive and fed with all my work – my drawing, my cooking, my cleaning. I've had my work featured in an important newspaper, I've given a speech to hundreds of people. I've made new friends, good friends, friends who really care about me. I've worn trousers. Trousers!

'Mama would be very proud of me,' I say firmly, knowing it's the truth.

She holds both my hands in hers. 'This is not goodbye, *Stellina*, it is *au revoir*, as your mother might have said. You know what this means?'

'Until we see each other again.'

She smiles. 'Yes. Until we see each other again.' She draws me into a warm hug and I hug her back, tight, tight, tight.

CHAPTER 26

In ancient Irish Brehon law there were special Bech Bretha *or* Bee Judgements *to protect bees. Destroying bees or bee colonies was considered a very serious offence.*

On Wednesday I'm in the kitchen talking to Sally when Mr Dalton walks in. I'm here to collect Jonty after study. My poor brother has to stay late to study with the Pennefeather boys every day from now on and he's not happy about it, although it's only for an extra hour. I think Papa's worried he'll run off with the circus if I don't supervise his return home. Papa might be right!

'Eliza, Mr and Mrs Pennefeather would like a word with you before you collect Jonty,' Mr Dalton says.

I look at him, trying not to sigh. I'm exhausted today. I slept really badly last night, thinking about everything and I could do without any more drama. 'Has Jonty done something wrong?' The mood Jonty's in at the moment I wouldn't be surprised.

'I don't think so,' he says. 'They don't seem angry.'

Angry? I feel like saying. I'm the one who should be angry with Mr Pennefeather for getting me in trouble with Papa.

'This way,' Mr Dalton leads me up the servants' stairway, into the hallway and up the marble stairs towards the sitting room.

Inside Mr and Mrs Pennefeather are sitting on the sofa, waiting for me.

Mr Pennefeather stands up as I walk in. 'Eliza,' he says, all smiles.

I don't smile back so he stops. Is it my imagination or have his cheeks gone red under his bushy beard?

'I believe I owe you an apology,' he says. 'I wasn't aware you hadn't told your father about your association with the Wildes' circus. I'm sorry if it put you in a difficult position.'

I soften. He does seem to be genuinely sorry and he has been good to Papa, to all of us. I need to remember that.

'It wasn't your fault, Mr Pennefeather,' I say. 'You weren't to know.'

'No hard feelings then?'

I cross my fingers behind my back. 'None.'

'Good. Now Mrs Pennefeather has a request.' He looks at

her. 'Go ahead, my dear.'

Mrs Pennefeather seems nervous and unsure of herself. She's playing with the edge of her lacy sleeve.

'I'll come straight to the point,' she says. 'I'd like to visit Henrietta Cottages.'

I stare at her, gobsmacked. 'Henrietta Cottages?' I repeat, wondering if I've heard right. 'But why?' I know it's a little rude, but it's out of my mouth before I can stop myself.

'I read Madam Ada's interview in *The Irish Times* this morning and she's quite right. We Dubliners do need to open our eyes to what's happening on our own doorsteps. I've looked at the photographs of Henrietta Cottages in the newspaper, but I want to see it for myself. Will you take me there, Eliza? Be my guide?'

It's a strange request but she seems quite determined. And as she was inspired by something Madam Ada wrote maybe some good will come of it. At the very least she might donate to the McAllisters' appeal.

'Yes,' I say. 'I'll take you.'

x x x

As we drive up Sackville Street in Mr Pennefeather's Benz Velo, Jonty has a huge beam on his face.

'Wait till George and Sid see this motor car,' he says. 'They'll be so excited. Do you think Mr Pennefeather will let them sit in it?'

I think of the boys' muddy legs and boots from playing in the street. 'Probably not,' I say. 'But they can look at it.'

Mr Pennefeather is sitting up front with Mr Dalton beside him. I'm in the back with Jonty and Mrs Pennefeather.

When we turn onto Dorset Street a gang of tenement children run along beside us, trying to keep up.

Mrs Pennefeather's eyes are wide. 'How can they run so fast with no boots on their feet?'

I wondered exactly the same thing when I first moved here. 'They're just used to it,' I say. I think of some of the Henrietta children I've seen with grubby bandages on their feet. 'They do get awful cuts sometimes,' I add.

As we turn right onto Henrietta Street, Mr Dalton points to our house and Mr Pennefeather pulls up right outside it. When he cuts the engine off I sit up in my leather seat and look around.

It's eerily silent. Everyone has stopped dead and is staring at us. The only noise is the cry of a few babies.

'Janey Mac,' I hear a boy say loudly. 'That's some motor car and is that Jonty Kane inside it?'

Within seconds we're surrounded by dozens of children calling Jonty's name.

'Jonty, give us a go!'

'Jonty, you lucky ducker!'

Some of the older boys and girls start clambering onto the running boards. There's a loud parp and they jump down in fright. Mr Pennefeather blows the horn once more.

'Off the motor car please, children,' he says. 'You'll damage it.'

The boys and girls start to run off. Some of the women come over and remind the children to mind their manners and not to be climbing on the gentleman's car.

'Sorry, Mister,' one of the women says to Mr Pennefeather.

'That's quite all right,' he says. 'Children will be children.'

As I climb out of the car after Mrs Pennefeather I spot Annie walking towards us.

'Eliza,' Annie says. 'What's going on? I heard the noise from the yard.'

'Annie, this is Mrs Pennefeather,' I say, introducing them. 'Jonty goes to school with her sons.'

I forgot to call Mrs Pennefeather Madam, but she doesn't seem to mind.

'Pleased to meet you,' Annie says politely, dropping into a small curtsy. I wonder if that's how she's been told to greet the ladies she works for in the big houses she cleans.

'And you, Annie,' says Mrs Pennefeather. 'Do you live on Henrietta Street?'

'Yes, Eliza's my best friend. And Jonty is great pals with my brothers George and Sid. That's them looking at the motor car with Jonty.' The boys are walking around the Benz Velo together, inspecting every inch of the wheels and bodywork.

'I've asked Eliza to give me a tour of Henrietta Cottages,' Mrs Pennefeather says. 'Perhaps you'd care to join me?'

Annie's face goes dark. 'A tour is it? Like you'd take of the Zoological Gardens or Dublin Castle? Six people died there last week including my friend's mam.'

'Please forgive me,' Mrs Pennefeather says quickly. 'You're quite right. I used the wrong word entirely. I'll be honest with you, Annie, until reading about the terrible tragedy I hadn't paid much attention to the housing situation in Dublin. I used to encounter sick tenement children when I was train-ing to be a nurse, poor mites. I'd rather forgotten about that part of my life until the circus benefit. And I read an inter-view with Madam Ada in the newspaper. It was a bit of a wake-up call.

'And now I'd like to try and help if I can. But in order to do that, to make others listen, I need to be able to tell people what I've seen first-hand.'

'And I'm sorry for snapping at you,' Annie says. 'It's been a difficult time. All right then, I'll show you the Cottages.' She hooks her right arm through mine. 'We'll do it together.'

'Thank you, Annie,' Mrs Pennefeather says. She turns towards the motor car where her husband and Mr Dalton have been talking. 'Mr Pennefeather,' she says, 'kindly take Jonty and Annie's brothers for a spin. You may collect me here in an hour.'

'Actually, my dear,' he says. 'I'd like to come with you if I may. Mr Dalton can drive the boys.'

x x x

Annie and I lead Mr and Mrs Pennefeather through the hallway of 16 Henrietta Street, towards the back yard. Mrs Pennefeather lingers for a moment, taking it all in.

I barely notice the battered walls these days and if the floor smells I fetch a bucket of water and a scrubbing brush and I wash it.

The yard is bustling as usual, full of women doing washing

and children playing. I notice Mrs Pennefeather is wearing stout brown walking shoes and is stepping over the pony droppings and bending under washing lines as if she does it every day. In fact I think I've underestimated Mrs Pennefeather; if anything it's her husband who seems ill at ease.

'That's our workshop,' I tell her, pointing it out as we pass. 'And through the archway is Henrietta Cottages.'

Annie and I lead them through the archway and turn right. We stop and look up the muddy laneway towards what was once Joseph's house.

'We'll start with number one Henrietta Cottages,' Annie says. 'The house that collapsed. It's behind that hoarding. Watch your feet. Don't want you tripping.' Mrs and Mr Pennefeather look down at the uneven surface which is still littered with stones and dust.

'My friends the McAllisters lived there,' Annie continues, pointing at the wooden hoarding as we draw closer. 'Mrs McAllister lost her life, poor woman. I broke this trying to help.' She points at the cast.

Mrs Pennefeather sighs. 'I did wonder about your arm. Terrible accident.'

'It weren't no accident,' Annie says. 'Not from what I've

heard. Mr Ryan in number two says the McAllisters' house was inspected a month ago. He got talking to the inspector afterwards and the man said he'd found sagging floor joists and something wrong with the front wall. It weren't plumb.'

'What's plumb?' I ask Annie.

'Straight,' she explains. 'The wall was bulging out a bit.'

'Surely workmen were sent in to fix it?' Mr Pennefeather asks.

Annie shakes her head. 'No. It got its cert and all. And not a thing fixed. Because you know who owns all those buildings, numbers one to six? Councillor Corrigan from Dublin Corporation.'

'But that can't be right,' Mr Pennefeather says.

Annie shrugs. 'Lots of these houses are owned by councillors and even Aldermen, it's no secret. But I'm sure you can check it in the library or somewhere.'

'I'll be sure to do that, Annie,' he says. 'Thank you.'

A group of children run past us, playing tag. A small girl falls and starts crying. She's cut one of her palms on the rubble from Joseph's house. She runs towards one of the small cottages wailing, followed by an older girl around Jonty's age.

'Mammy,' the little one cries. 'Mammy!'

A woman appears in one of the doorways. The outside of the cottage is almost black with mud, the roof is sagging and several tiles are missing. The brickwork around one of the two windows has collapsed and has been patched up with a mishmash of old bricks, stones and newspaper.

The woman bends down to soothe the girl. Her clothes are almost as ragged as her daughter's, but at least she has a pair of battered boots on her feet. The little girl's feet are bare.

'Let's get that hand washed under the tap,' she tells the girl.

'I'll take her, Mam,' the older girl says.

As the two girls walk past us together Mrs Pennefeather asks the woman, 'Is she all right?'

The woman nods. 'She'll live.' She looks Mrs Pennefeather up and down. 'Lost, are you?'

I smile to myself, remembering Annie's exact same question the day we met.

'I was wondering if I might see inside your cottage,' Mrs Pennefeather says.

The woman's eyes narrow. 'You some sort of inspector? Or a journalist?'

'No, just an interested citizen.'

'A do-gooder like?'

'That's right,' Annie says, jumping in. 'Mrs Pennefeather wants to see the tenements for herself so she can change things.'

The woman gives a dry laugh. 'Change things? I'd like to see you try, Missus.'

She looks at Annie carefully, taking in her cast. 'You Tall Joe's girl?'

Annie blushes. 'His friend, yes.'

The woman sighs. 'Go on then if it makes you happy,' she says to Mrs Pennefeather. 'But don't get too close to the baby in bed. He's right sick, so he is.'

'Thank you.' Mrs Pennefeather dips her head to walk through the low doorway, followed by Mr Pennefeather. I step forward to go in too, but Annie puts her hand on my arm.

'Best let them look on their own,' she says.

As Annie and the woman talk about Peter and Minnie McAllister and how they're getting on, I take a quick peek through the door. The inside of the cottage is dark and damp and a small smoky fire is spluttering in the grate. There's no furniture at all, no table, no chairs, not even a stool.

The floor is part stone, part earth and the only piece of it that is covered is the far right-hand wall where piles of straw have old flour sacks and pieces of old coat thrown over them. It must be where they all sleep.

Mr and Mrs Pennefeather are standing over what seems to be a bundle of old rags. There's a tiny sound from the rags, a whimper, and I realise with horror that it's the sick baby.

A family lives like this? Like *this*? Circus animals with thick fur should sleep on straw, not people! Something rises up through me, shame and pity and despair, and I try to swallow it down and blink back the tears that are threatening to spill down my cheeks.

When I turn back around I feel Annie's eyes on me. She gives me a look and I know I can't cry so I pull myself together. It's not the woman's fault that her family has so little and I mustn't make her feel bad about it. I know tenement people are proud and strong, Annie showed me that. They are doing their best and they don't like others feeling sorry for them.

When Mrs Pennefeather comes out of the cottage, followed by Mr Pennefeather, her eyes are glittering with tears, just like mine were. She takes a deep breath. 'I believe your baby has diphtheria. You must get to her the hospital immediately.'

'He,' the woman says. 'James.'

Mr Pennefeather's face is pale and he's gone very quiet. He reaches into his pocket, takes out his wallet and presses some notes into the woman's hand. 'Please take this,' he says. 'I hope it will help.'

The woman nods and stares down at the notes. She seems a little stunned. I'm not surprised, because there's at least five pounds in her hand.

'Thank you, Sir,' she says. 'God bless you both.' She walks back into her house.

Mrs Pennefeather opens her mouth to say something to me and Annie, but she seems to be finding it hard to find words. 'I'm so sorry,' she says eventually. 'We didn't know.' She gestures at the cottages on the laneway. 'These houses… These conditions…' She shakes her head. 'We didn't know.'

'Well you do now,' I say firmly. 'The people who live here are brave, so brave. And now you have a chance to be brave too, Mrs Pennefeather. Madam Ada always told me that, to be brave no matter what.'

She nods. 'You're right. And I'll try to follow her advice. She sounds like a wonderful person, this Madam Ada. There must be something we can do. What's the point of having so much money if we can't help others? Are you with me, Mr Pennefeather?'

He smiles. 'I am, my dear. Absolutely.'

She smiles back. Her eyes flash and her whole face lights up. And then I see it, she really is beautiful. She's practically glowing. And Mr Pennefeather is gazing at her as if she's the Mona Lisa.

'And now I wish to visit your father please, Eliza,' she says. 'There's something I need to talk to him about.'

CHAPTER 27

There are around one hundred bee and pollinator species in Ireland and twenty-one of these species are bumblebees. There is a species of bee that is found only on the Aran Islands. It is called the Bombus muscorum var allenellus.

'I believe you caused quite a commotion around Henrietta Street this afternoon, Eliza,' Papa says that evening over dinner. 'What with the Pennefeathers' motor car, not to mention their visit to Henrietta Cottages.'

I look at him, but he doesn't seem cross.

'Mrs Pennefeather was most taken with your appetite for social reform,' he adds. 'She was impressed with your friend Annie too.'

'What does that mean?' Jonty says. 'Social reform?'

'Helping people,' Papa says. 'Mrs Pennefeather insisted on reading me Eliza's speech from the benefit too.'

'My speech?' I say, a little confused. 'Where did she get it?'

'It was printed in this morning's *Irish Times,* along with an interview with Madam something or other from the circus. A bee charmer apparently.' He stops for a moment. 'Your mother was always fond of bees, wasn't she?'

I nod. 'She loved them. She told me her name means "bee" in Greek.'

'I never knew that,' he says. 'About your mother's name, I mean.' He stops for a moment. 'How does this bee charming work exactly?'

'I know the secret,' Jonty pipes up. 'Can I tell him, Eliza?'

As Jonty explains Madam Ada's secret, I listen, my heart squeezing. I miss Madam Ada and the circus so much.

When Jonty's finished Papa surprises me by saying, 'How interesting, Jonty. It sounds like quite the skill.' His dark mood of the last few days seems to have lifted for now. But I'm nervous it will come back again.

'Can I go outside and play with George and the gang now, Papa?' Jonty asks. He's clearly noticed Papa's good mood too and is taking advantage of it.

'Yes, just for a little while.'

Jonty runs out the door, forgetting to close it behind him. I get up and do it for him and then start clearing away the dinner plates.

When I've finished Papa says 'Could you read me the interview with the bee charmer now, Eliza. If you wouldn't mind.'

'I'd be happy to, Papa.' I wasn't expecting that question. Delighted, I sit back down, pick up the newspaper and flick through the pages until I see a large photo of Madam Ada staring out at me, the black and white newsprint making her eyes look even more dark and mysterious. One of her queen bees is sitting on her palm. My heart gives another little pang. What I wouldn't give to see the circus in person.

I start reading, beginning with the headline. *'Circus Benefit Raises Thirty-Four Pounds for Families After Tenement Disaster.*

Madam Ada Wilde, wife of circus proprietor Mr Zozimus Wilde and an accomplished performer in her own right, organised a special benefit show in aid of the families of the tenement disaster.

'Joseph McAllister is a treasured member of our circus family,' *she explained from her golden circus caravan. She speaks in a rich Italian accent and breaks into Italian words from time to time.*

'When I heard about the disaster, the collapse of his house and the death of his mother, I knew I must do something, for him and

the other families in that house.

So I talked to the circus artists and we all decided to put together a special performance featuring some new acts. We had a packed house and I am grateful for the generosity of everyone who attended and to my fellow performers who gave their time freely and without question.'

Madam Wilde has a rather unusual background. When pressed, she admitted that she is a member of the ancient Visconti family of Milan, quite the lineage. 'Our family crest is a serpent,' she joked. 'Circus was il mio destino, my destiny.'

She met her husband while singing in London with an Italian touring opera company and she said it was love at first sight, for him! Her act – riding a white stallion while covered in honey bees – is world renowned. It needs to be seen to be believed! This reporter witnessed it at the benefit performance and it was breath-taking. She also treated the audience to her remarkable bell-like voice. She has transformed her circus act into a cultural art form.

'Enough about me,' she says, modestly deflecting any further questions about her fascinating background. 'I wish to talk about the tenements. There is poverty in Milan and in London but I have never seen anything like the poverty in Dublin. The land-lords ought to be ashamed of themselves.

'Some of the flats I have seen are not fit for anyone. I would not allow my circus dogs or lions live there. Not even my snakes.

'I am calling on the good people of Dublin to open your eyes. Go and see the tenements for yourselves, they are right on your doorstep. And then do something – demand change. Talk to anyone in power who will listen. People can change the world if they rally together.

'Demand an inquiry into the Henrietta Cottages disaster. Demand safe and clean homes for every family in Dublin in the future. You have a voice. Use it. Allora! Now!'

'Quite the speech. All delivered with an unusual spirit and warmth. This is a woman who truly cares about the underdog.

'Before the end of the interview, she made me promise to do my best to raise awareness of the tenement collapse. I gave her my solemn oath. Madam Wilde is not a lady to be trifled with!

'Mr Zozimus Wilde's Travelling Circus will give its last Dublin performance on Saturday 24th June before it travels back to London the following week. Don't miss it!

I see now what had driven Mrs Pennefeather to visit Henrietta Cottages – Madam Ada's stirring words!

Papa has gone very quiet. I put the paper down.

'What did you think of the interview, Papa?'

'Interesting,' he says simply, twisting his signet ring on his finger. 'Now please leave me to my thoughts, Eliza. I need to be alone.'

x x x

The following morning I get up early and I'm surprised to find Papa already sitting at the window in his favourite arm-chair, staring out at the Henrietta Street rooftops.

His clothes are dishevelled and his collar is loose. He can't have been there all night, can he?

'Papa,' I say. 'Are you all right?'

He turns his head, slowly, as if it's a little stiff.

'Eliza, wake up your brother, please. I wish to speak to you both.'

Jonty isn't happy at being woken up at six in the morning, moaning and clamping his pillow over his head.

'Papa's waiting for us in the everything room. Come on!'

'What does he want?'

'I don't know.'

'Does he look cross?'

'No. But he does look tired so please hurry up.'

'He's tired? You're waking me up in the middle of the

night, Eliza!'

'It's six in the morning and the sun's shining, Jonty. Get a move on.'

'It feels like the middle of the night,' he grumbles, finally rolling out of bed. 'And what's the point of getting up? All I've got is stupid school, school, school.'

X X X

'So what is it, Papa?' I say. Jonty's standing beside me scowling, still only half-dressed.

Papa begins 'I may have been wrong about your circus. Madam Wilde sounds, well, she sounds like a lady of substance.'

I hold my breath, waiting for what he's going to say next.

'Jonty did not have a chance to make his farewells. I will allow you to both say goodbye to your circus friends on Sunday if you'd like to.'

'Magic!' Jonty says. He jumps down and gives Papa a big hug.

'Thank you, Papa.' I have no idea which part of Madam Ada's interview made him change his mind but whatever it was, hallelujah for *The Irish Times* and Mrs Pennefeather.

X X X

That afternoon George kindly delivers a message to Madam Ada to let her know we'll be visiting on Sunday.

A little later George hands me back a cream envelope. 'Here you go, Eliza. This is for you.' I open it. There's a tiny gold bee on the top of the cream correspondence card.

Darling Eliza, it reads in beautiful cursive writing. *We cannot wait to see you. It will be chaos up at the circus field but we have a plan. Meet us up there at three in the afternoon. Yours, Madam Ada and Albert.*

CHAPTER 28

Beekeeping is both an art and a science. Only those who respect the nature of these magnificent creatures will succeed. It is for the brain as well as the hands and feet.

'I've got a plan,' Jonty says as we walk towards the circus compound on Sunday. 'I'm going to leave school and run away with the circus.'

There's such determination on his face that I don't laugh.

'I'll miss Madam Ada and Albert too,' I say. 'And at least the circus will be back again next year. Albert said they visit Dublin every June.'

'A whole year?' Jonty stops walking and stares at me. 'I can't wait a whole year to see Pepper and the other dogs again.'

I shrug. 'Maybe Papa will let you get a cat.'

Jonty scrunches up his nose. 'Not the same. You can't train cats. They just sniff at you and run off. Different kind of animal all together, cats.'

I smile. If anyone knows, it's Jonty. He's tried training all kinds of animals over the years.

In an ideal world I'd love to run away with the circus too. But I know I can't leave Papa to fend for himself. And the honest truth is, much as I love the circus, I don't want to leave Annie either. She has a lot on her hands at the moment, what with working and looking after Minnie and Peter. But despite everything, she never stops smiling. She really is a wonder.

x x x

As we approach the circus field I get a fright. The caravans are all still there, but the big top has disappeared.

We both stop dead and stare at the large circle of brown grass where the tent used to stand. How could something so solid and alive simply vanish?

'I guess it's true then,' Jonty says. 'They really are going.'

'Over here, 'Liza!' Albert is waving at me. He's standing beside the bee wagon with Madam Ada.

As we walk towards them, I feel a rush of happiness at seeing them again. Jonty throws his arms around Albert.

'Albert!' he says. 'I missed you!'

Albert pulls back and rubs the top of Jonty's head. 'Here now, little man. All good, all good.'

Madam Ada is smiling at me. 'Ready to go?'

'Go where?' I ask.

'To the Honey Garden of course. I have to settle in my bees and say goodbye to them. I was hoping you and your brother might help me. And yes, before you ask, Pepper can come too, Jonty.'

Jonty gives her a huge grin.

x x x

As we ride over the bumps on Dorset Street I sing my heart out to the bees. It's my last trip with them and I want to do my very best to make them comfortable and happy. I guess I'm singing for Madam Ada and Albert too – a farewell song.

Au clair de la lune, Mon ami Pierrot, Prête-moi ta plume Pour écrire un mot.

As I sing, I can hear the bees buzzing in their hives, a gentle, restful hum.

'You're going home, little bees,' I tell them. 'Not far now.'

Jonty is sitting up front with Madam Ada, Albert and Pepper. It's a bit of a squish, but they all just about fit. My brother's holding Daisy's reins and every now and then he says, 'Giddy up, Daisy, there's a girl,' loudly, like he's been driving horses all his life.

When we reach the Honey Garden, Albert opens the gates and Madam Ada helps Jonty drive Daisy inside. I breathe in the heady, sweet smell of the flowers, trying to remember every single sight and smell of this trip and lock it away in my heart.

Albert unhooks the back of the wagon and I climb down. I look over at the hives in the garden. Every little wooden roof is covered with a piece of heavy black material.

I hear Madam Ada's voice beside me. 'It's mourning cloth, *Stellina*. They're in mourning for Joseph's mother.'

I must look puzzled by this – and I am, mystified – so she adds 'When something important happens, a birth, a marriage or a death, especially a death, you must tell the bees. If you do not they may leave the hive and never return. And if someone dies, they like to wear mourning garb. It's an ancient tradition and who are we to meddle with tradition?'

A worker bee flies over and lands on my shoulder. I let her rest there. The faint hum of her wings is soothing.

'Today we must tell my bees about their new beekeeper,' Madam Ada adds. 'And their new bee charmer.'

'A new beekeeper?' I ask her. 'Is it Albert?'

She smiles, her eyes twinkling in the sun light. 'No, it is

you, *Stellina*. You are the chosen one. Will you be their new keeper and look after my bees for me? It's usually Joseph's job and he will help you when he's well again but-'

My heart swells. 'I'd love to, Madam Ada!' The fact that she trusts me – me! – with her precious bees. The very idea of it makes me happy. I can deal with Papa's thoughts on the matter later. Right now I'm going to embrace my new job as Madam Ada's beekeeper.

She smiles. 'I was hoping you'd say that.' She walks over to the wagon and takes out a large canvas bag. I follow her.

'These are for you, *Stellina*.' She reaches into the bag and hands me a pair of thick white gloves and a hat with a veil attached, like the one I'd seen Joseph wearing when he was helping with her bees. 'Wear these when you are near the hives just in case.'

I put them on. The mesh of the veil darkens the world, making it look softer.

'Albert, can you help Jonty put on his gloves and veil?' she asks, passing him the bag. 'And if you boys could then carry the hives to their resting places against the wall, that would be wonderful.'

'Of course, Aunt Ada,' Albert says. 'And you look like a real beekeeper now, 'Liza.'

As Albert and Jonty get ready to carry over the first hive from the back of the wagon, Madam Ada takes my hand and leads me towards the other hives.

'*Andiamo,*' she says. 'Come.'

She knocks firmly with her knuckles on the first hive we come to. The bees inside start to buzz. A few workers fly out of the entrance to see what the commotion is.

She lifts the black material, leans in towards the hive and says in a low, rhythmic voice: 'I have news, dear bees. I must take my leave of you. But you are now in the hands of my *Stellina*. She will care for you until we meet again. She will visit you once a week and check your hives have not come to any harm.'

'*Stellina*, say hello to my dear bees, so they may hear your voice.'

I move closer to the hive. 'Hello, bees, I am honoured to meet you,' I say, trying to keep my voice low and calm like Madam Ada's. 'My name is Eliza Kane. I will do my very best to keep you safe from harm.'

We move to the next hive and do the same thing.

'Do you have your sketchbook, *Stellina*?' Madam Ada asks.

'You might want to write down the Queens' names so you remember them. This hive belongs to Queen Isabella.'

She introduces me to every hive, ending up with the hives Albert and Jonty have just lifted into place. At every one I write down the Queen's name carefully. There are twelve in total and it takes quite a while.

Jonty looks a bit baffled by it all, but unusually for him, he simply watches silently. After a little while, he joins Albert and Pepper who are playing on the grass.

When we've finished our hive visits Madam Ada says 'Here is what you must do every week. The bees will have plenty of honey to keep them going all winter. Check the hives are all upright and the lids are safe and secure. If it gets cold or snows, knock the ice gently off the hives and make sure the entrance is not blocked by snow or dead bees. Over the winter it is too cold for them to fly so they will cluster together to keep warm with the queen in the middle.'

I jot down some notes as she talks, not wanting to forget anything.

'Knock on the hives to let them know you are there and if all is well they will buzz back at you. It is a lot to remember but you can ask Joseph if you forget anything.' She stops and smiles at me.

'And by next summer they will know you like an old friend, *Stellina*. And I can train you to perform as a circus bee charmer if you are brave enough and your father allows it. You have all the makings of a wonderful bee charmer already.'

Me? I'm the new bee charmer she was talking about? I'm not sure about that idea. I'm still a bit nervous of the bees and the thought of them crawling around my throat – yikes! But maybe I'll feel differently in a year. And besides who knows if Papa will actually let me? For now I just say 'Thank you, Madam Ada.'

'You're circus family now,' she says. 'You can call me Aunt Ada if you like.'

My heart does a little skip. Circus family? I like that. I like that a lot!

'Thank you, Aunt Ada,' I repeat with a smile.

After we're finished, I take off my veil and gloves and we walk nearer to Albert and Jonty who are playing with Pepper at the far end of the garden, throwing a stick for her to fetch.

'Join me.' Madam Ada sits on the lion bench under the pagoda and pats the wood beside her. It reminds me of sitting outside the hospital with her. It seems like years ago, but it's only a few days. But what a few days!

'I will miss you, Stellina,' she begins. 'But we will see each other very soon. The time will fly until next summer, you'll see. But in the meantime I have something for you.' She puts her hand in her skirt pocket, takes out an envelope and hands it to me. 'Your earnings and Jonty's earnings. And a little extra for your father's operation.'

I open it and look inside. Five blue bank notes. From the Provincial Bank of Ireland Limited. Five whole pounds. A fortune!

'I can't take this,' I say. 'It's too much. And even if we do have the money, Papa is refusing to have the operation.'

'Why do you think that is, *Stellina*?'

I shrug. 'I honestly don't know. He says he's scared of completely losing his sight, but that seems to be happening anyway. He's so sad all the time. Sorry, I don't mean to spoil our last day together.'

'You are not spoiling anything, you are being honest. And it sounds like your father's heart is broken. He has lost the love of his life, but he has also lost his way, I fear. Try talking to him, telling him how you feel. Be brave, *Stellina*.'

'I'm scared,' I admit. 'But you're right, I have to try. Mama was the one I talked to about difficult things. I wish she was here now.'

'But she is with you, my darling.' She kisses her fingers and rests her hand gently over my heart.

I close my eyes for a second and think of Mama's kind eyes and honey scent and the way she used to brush my hair out of my eyes with her fingers. I'm not sure if I'm imagining it, but suddenly I hear Mama's voice in my head. 'I am always with you, my darling girl. Always.' I give a deep sigh, a happy sigh with a little 'Ah' at the end of it. Then I open my eyes.

Madam Ada takes her hand away. '*Stellina?* Are you all right?'

I nod. 'Yes. Just remembering Mama.'

'It is good to remember the people we love. Now, I'm afraid our time together must end. I have a circus to pack up.'

As I put the envelope Madam Ada gave me in my pocket my fingers rub against something metal. I almost forgot!

'This is for you, Madam Ada,' I say a little shyly. 'I mean Aunt Ada.' I hand her my locket on its silver chain. 'My mother gave it to me for my thirteenth birthday, but I want you to have it. There's something inside.'

'I am honoured, Eliza.' She opens the locket carefully and looks at the two small miniatures I painted, one of me and Jonty, and the other of Albert.

'*Oh mio Dio*, what portraits! So lifelike!' There are tears in her eyes. 'It's the most beautiful present I have ever been given.'

'Your circus children,' I say. 'So you won't forget us, Aunt Ada.'

She puts her hand on my cheek. '*Impossibile, Stellina*! *Impossibile!*' She kisses the locket. 'Will you help me put it on?'

I fasten it around her neck and, when it's nestling against her skin, she places her fingers on it. 'I will cherish my locket forever.'

X X X

On the way back to the circus field Albert joins me in the back of the wagon, while Jonty sits up front again and drives Daisy, Pepper by his side.

'I was thinking I could write to you, 'Liza,' Albert says as we ride up the quays. 'If you wouldn't mind.'

I smile. 'Mind? I'd love that, Albert! And I promise to write back.'

He grins. 'I'll address it to Miss 'Liza Kane. The Little Bee Charmer of Henrietta Street.'

CHAPTER 29

Archaeologists have found honey buried in Ancient Egyptian tombs that is still edible. Honey is the only food on earth that does not spoil or go off.

Walking along the quays with Jonty on the way home from the circus, I think about what Madam Ada said about being brave and talking to Papa. She was right, I must talk to him about his eyes. I can't put it off any longer.

'Jonty,' I say, 'Madam Ada gave me our wages. I want to give it to Papa for his eye operation. How do you feel about that?'

'All of it?'

'Yes. Every penny.'

He goes quiet for a long moment. Then he stops and stares at the Liffey. Its surface is dancing in the sun. 'Remember the day I saved Pepper?' he says finally.

I nod. 'I'll never forget it. You were amazing, Jonty.'

He smiles. 'It felt good. Helping Pepper I mean. So my

answer is yes. I would have worked at the circus for nothing. Best fun ever.'

'Thanks, Jonty. Now we just have to persuade Papa to have that operation.'

x x x

As we walk in the door, Papa is in his usual place, sitting in the armchair, his face towards the window. His eyes are so milky now I have no idea how much he can see.

He turns towards us. 'Did you say your goodbyes to your friends at the circus?'

'Yes,' I say. I decide to launch straight in, before I get the chance to change my mind. 'Papa, our wages from the circus will cover your eye operation.'

He gives a hollow laugh. 'You can't possibly have earned five pounds.'

'We did. Madam Ada gave us some extra. It's all in this envelope.' I place it on the small card table in front of Papa.

He leaves it sitting there. The room goes quiet. Then Jonty breaks the silence.

'Papa, if you have the operation I'll stay at the Pennefeathers' and work really, really hard. As hard as any boy has ever worked. I'll get top marks in all my exams and even go to college.'

'And I'll do whatever you want me to do,' I say. 'I don't need to go back to art college, I can run the studio. We just want you to be able to see again, Papa, so you can paint, and do your drama, and go out to your club with Mr Pennefeather.'

'And be happy again,' Jonty adds. 'And maybe then we could get a dog. Not a big one, just a small one. George says Jack Russells make great rat catchers. I saw one yesterday in the yard. A rat I mean. Huge it was ...'

'Jonty!' I say, giving him a warning look and he stops going on about the rat.

Papa stares out the window again. But he doesn't look happy. His face is turning from white to red and his chest is starting to heave up and down, like he's been running.

He turns towards us. 'Out!' he shouts. 'Both of you.' He points at the door. 'Out!'

'But Papa-' I say shocked.

'I don't want to talk to either of you right now. Out!' He jumps to his feet, knocking the card table over. He steps forward, falling over it and tumbling to the ground.

'Papa!' I go to help him, but he shouts at me 'I can do it, leave me alone!'

Jonty looks at me, his eyes scared. Papa sometimes shouts, but I've never seen him this furious.

'Sorry, Papa,' I say, as I take Jonty's arm and pull him out of the room with me. As I close the door behind us I hear a wooden screech from inside, and then another. I think Papa is kicking the table across the room.

'Come on, Jonty,' I say. 'Let's go outside.'

Jonty looks at me, tears in his eyes. 'I'm not getting a dog, am I?'

'One day you'll have your own dog again,' I say. 'I promise.'

x x x

We stay out as long as we can. Luckily George and Sid are playing cowboys outside with Peter and Minnie so Jonty joins in. I sit on the front steps and watch them. By eight o'clock I'm so hungry I could eat a horse and my stomach is rumbling.

We can't spend the night on the street. I'm sure Annie would take us in if it came to that, but maybe Papa has calmed down by now. I have to chance it for Jonty's sake. I know Papa's outburst frightened him and I want be brave, to face Papa again, to show Jonty that you have to do difficult things sometimes, things that make you scared.

But boy, am I terrified when we walk up the stairs towards our flat! Of Papa's anger, yes, but also of the future. What will become of us if Papa goes completely blind?

Eliza, I tell myself, you can do this. Whatever happens, you will be all right. I remember Madam Ada's words: 'Be brave, *Stellina*.'

My hands are shaking a little as I open the door but Papa isn't in his chair. He's sitting at the dinner table and it's set for the three of us. The knives and forks are a bit crooked, but he's done his best. In the middle of the table in a bowl are the three eggs I boiled for us last night, along with a loaf of bread and some butter.

Jonty looks at the table and then back at me.

'Eliza?' he whispers. 'Are we supposed to sit down?'

'Yes, yes,' Papa says. The fire has gone out of his voice and I feel a wave of relief. 'What are you waiting for?' he adds. 'Sit, sit.'

We take our seats. Silence again.

'Will I cut the bread, Papa?' I ask.

'I'd slice my finger off if I tried. My blasted eyes.' He gives a deep sigh.

As I cut the bread, Papa continues to talk. 'A strange thing happened this afternoon. A bee flew in the open window and settled on my hand. It stayed there for several seconds and it reminded me of your mother and how she used to put honey on any skin rashes or burns. She said they were the cleverest animals in the world, bees.

'It set me thinking. She was an intelligent woman, your mother. A woman of science who also believed in magic. Even towards the end she still believed the world was a place full of wonder. She made me promise to listen to you both and support your dreams.'

He rubs his hands over his face and gives another sigh.

'I haven't been doing that, children. Instead I've listened to my own dark thoughts, my fears of losing my sight completely and not being able to see your smiling faces every morning. Because it's your smiles that keep me going.

'I've been angry and I've been scared, so scared of the doctor cutting into my eyeball and getting it wrong. I'm terrified of losing whatever sight I have left and going completely blind. And that's the truth of it. But I'm even more scared of losing you both – your love and your respect. And I'm sorry for shouting at you earlier. I was angry and frustrated and I took it out on you. It wasn't right and I am so sorry for scaring you both. I wasn't myself.'

He sits up in his chair. 'I've made a decision, I'll do it, I'll have the operation. As soon as possible.'

'Papa!' I drop the bread knife, run towards him and throw my arms around him. Jonty follows me. We squeeze and squeeze and squeeze until Papa begs us to stop.

X X X

Over dinner we tell him about our trip to the Honey Garden.

'I drove Daisy,' Jonty says. 'She's one of Madam Ada's horses. And I played with Pepper for ages and ages. It was magic.'

'And I told the bees I'd be looking after them for Madam Ada, if that's all right, Papa,' I say. 'It's only once a week. As soon as Joseph is better he can take over.'

He goes quiet for a moment and I hold my breath. 'Yes, Eliza. If Madam Ada needs help, then you can be her bee-keeper.'

I don't ask him about bee charming. I figure that's a question for a much later day. But for the first time since Mama died I start to feel hopeful about our future.

CHAPTER 30

A bee colony could continue to thrive and produce new bees forever as long as it is not threatened by predators, diseases or extreme weather. It could in theory become an immortal or everlasting colony.

A MONTH LATER

'So this is Henrietta Street,' Papa says. It's his first time outside since the bandages came off yesterday and I'm giving him a guided tour of the area, with Jonty and our new dog, Lucky, a little black and white scrap of a thing with the cutest face ever.

Jonty and George found him on the street and Jonty begged so hard to keep him that Papa gave in. He lives in the workshop most of the time, keeping me company while I'm drawing and painting. Sleeps there too. We have no idea what kind of dog he is – a bit of everything, Papa says – but he's got the sweetest nature and Jonty is utterly in love with him.

Today Jonty has Lucky on a lead and is taking his training very seriously. 'Sit,' he tells the little dog as we stand on the top of the steps outside 16 Henrietta Street. Lucky ignores him at first and Jonty gently pushes down his bottom. 'This is sit, Lucky,' he says patiently.

'What a busy place,' Papa says. His eyes sweep the street from the fine King's Inns buildings through the gates at the top of the street, to the noisy junction with Bolton Street at the bottom of the street, just past our building. He takes in the girls playing skipping on the pavement, the women chatting on the doorsteps, babies on their hips, the screams, the cries, the laughter, all of it.

He smiles when he spots George and Sid kicking their precious new leather ball on the cobblestones, a present from Mrs Pennefeather. She's visited Henrietta Street and Cottages several times over the last few weeks to see Papa.

'Yes, it is, Papa,' I say, proudly. 'A busy, muddy, happy place. Over eight hundred people live on this street and we all look out for each other.'

He whistles. 'That's a lot of people. I'd like to see the workshop and Henrietta Cottages next.'

And that's the best bit – *see*. Because after many weeks of wondering and hoping and, let's be honest, lots of days of grumpiness, impatience and irritation on his part, he's not a good patient – Papa can see.

'Are you sure, Papa? It's still very dusty at the Cottages.'

He nods. 'I'm sure.'

We visit the workshop first. Looking around inside he doesn't seem all that impressed. 'Have the windows always been broken?'

'Yes.'

'Which affects the light for our illuminations,' Papa says. 'I'll be back at work on Monday and I shall be having words with the landlord. He took advantage of my lack of sight when I viewed the place.'

While I padlock the workshop door Papa goes quiet. He seems sad.

'Everything all right, Papa?' I ask him. 'We can go back inside if you like.'

He looks at me, his eyes soft. 'I am so sorry, poppet. I had no idea...' He waves his hand around the yard. 'All of this, it's hard to take in. And I know we live in relative luxury compared to other families in the building. I met your friend Annie earlier when she was cleaning the stairs. I asked her to show me her flat and she kindly did. The broken floorboards are a disgrace. What do you think about giving them one of our rugs? It would help with the draughts.'

'I think it's a lovely idea, Papa. Annie will be over the moon. She's been very good to me and Jonty.'

'And to me,' Papa adds. 'Charming young lady.' While he's been laid up, Annie has been visiting Papa, sitting with him and talking to him. She even changed his bandages one evening as I had a deadline for a piece of artwork – my first portrait commission – of a cat!

A lady called Mrs Beamish had spotted my illuminated poem on the Pennefeathers' wall. I'd decorated the border with some of Mr Pennefeather's favourite things, his motor car, wine bottles and Stilton cheese (Papa's idea) and books. I'd also added some animals to fill up the space. Luckily he hadn't spotted the tiny black sewer rat on the motor car's running board. I painted that in while I was still angry with him.

Anyway, Mrs Beamish asked me to paint her Siamese, Minerva. I wasn't sure at first – it was a strange request – but it turned out to be fun, although Minerva didn't like staying still for more than one minute. She was far more interested in climbing Mrs Beamish's curtains. Mrs Beamish said I captured Minerva's wild, free spirit perfectly and she has recommended me to all her friends for pet portraits.

Lucky is straining on his lead, pulling Jonty through the arch, so we follow him.

'This is Henrietta Cottages, Papa,' I say as we walk up the laneway. 'The McAllisters' house was up there.' I nod towards what's left of Joseph's old house, the back wall.

Papa walks towards the wooden hoarding. 'Tragic,' he says. 'Six souls lost.'

'And a cat,' Jonty reminds us. 'Poor Raven.'

'And a cat,' Papa says. 'And for what? Money! The greed of the landlords. Something must be done. They can't get away with it. Not while I have breath in my body and sight in my eyes.' He pulls himself up taller. 'Screw your courage to the sticking place and we'll not fail.'

'Sticking what?' I look at him, confused.

He smiles. '*Macbeth*. It means tighten up your courage, be brave.'

Strange quotes from Mr Shakespeare? Hurrah, Papa is back!

X X X

As we walk back through the arch, Lucky scampering towards the yard and pulling Jonty along behind him, something occurs to me. 'Papa, I know Henrietta Street isn't perfect, but the people here are so kind. And Jonty loves it, especially now he has Lucky. We're not leaving, are we? I'd really like to stay.'

'Leaving?' Papa says. 'Absolutely not! It may not be perfect, as you say, but it's home now. We stay. And we work together to make Henrietta Street better for everyone. Besides, I'm not sure we'd find anywhere else that will take those two tearaways.'

I look at Jonty and Lucky. Jonty is trying to teach the puppy to stand on his hind legs and dance, like Pepper does. He's not having much success but from the laughter and the yapping, they're loving it anyway.

As I stand there, watching, a worker bee buzzes into the yard and hovers beside me for a moment.

'Home,' I hear a soft voice say. And then she flies away.

EPILOGUE

16 Henrietta Street,

Dublin,

Ireland,

The World,

The Universe.

Friday, 1 September 1911

Dear Albert,

I hope you get this letter safely. Jonty says to give Pepper a big hug from him and lots of chicken treats. He has a new puppy called Lucky and he's going to teach him all kinds of circus tricks.

Before I forget, can you thank Madam Ada for the beekeeping book? It was delivered last week. It's full of fascinating bee information and Jonty wants to read it next. He loves learning new facts about animals!

Did you know that archaeologists have found honey

in Egyptian tombs? And it is still edible! Imagine! Annie loved that fact – she's fascinated by the pyramids.

Speaking of Annie, you'll never guess what happened last Sunday. Joseph only went and proposed to Annie in the Honey Garden! He asked me to help him set it all up. We covered the pagoda and lion bench in a garland of flowers – all yellow, Annie's favourite colour – and while Annie was sitting on the bench he dropped down on one knee and asked her to marry him.

Annie told him not to be so daft, that she's far too young for that kind of nonsense. 'In the future then?' he asked her. She just laughed. But I know she was secretly delighted. It's the talk of Henrietta Street!

I made sure to tell the bees the news of the proposal and Annie's reply. If they ever do marry (and I think they will!) I'll be sure to give the bees some wedding cake.

I have news too. From next Monday I will be back at art college. Yippee! I can't wait! Papa has taken on Annie's brother, George, as a messenger boy and assistant – it turns out George is rather good at art and Papa is delighted with him. Papa has lots of work coming in and Mrs Pennefeather has asked him to be on her Dublin

Housing Committee so he's very busy, but he likes it that way.

They're trying to build good houses with affordable rent for Dublin workers and their families. They've already raised enough to build three cottages. One of them will go to Joseph and his family. Isn't that terrific? Papa's even found time to start amateur dramatics again. He's going to be King Lear soon!

Jonty is back at school with the Pennefeather boys. He says he hates, it but he's started bringing science books home to read at night for fun. He's aiming to take his college entrance exams a year early so he can get away from Harry and Theo. Their tutor, Mr Stephens, says there's a good chance he'll make it into veterinary college on a scholarship as his grades are so good. I think my little brother will make a brilliant veterinarian!

One final thing, Albert. Tell Aunt Ada that Queen Regina and all the bees send their kindest and most loving regards.

Your little bee charmer,

'Liza XXX

IRELAND AND DUBLIN
IN 1911

*T*he Little Bee Charmer of Henrietta Street *is fiction, but* there is lots of real history in the book. The Dublin tenements existed and sadly sometimes tenement buildings really did collapse, although Henrietta Cottages, where the book's collapse happens, is a fictional laneway. Henrietta Street is a real place you can visit to this day, although number sixteen was knocked down a long time ago; and bee charmers really were a part of travelling circuses in the past.

In case, like me, you are a very curious person and are interested in the real history that inspired this story, I put together these notes for you.

WHAT WERE THE TENEMENTS?

The tenements were flats where many families lived in one room or group of rooms, often in poor conditions. They were

Tenements on Chancery Lane, Dublin 1913 and some of the people who lived there.

often carved out of larger buildings, such as grand Georgian homes.

These days we take things like running water, toilets and showers for granted, but in 1911, 20,000 Dublin families lived in one-room tenements in the inner city. Sometimes children, parents and grandparents would all live in this one room; some families even had a lodger too.

Dublin had the worst housing conditions of any city in Ireland or Britain at the time and children often got sick or died because of the conditions. The death rate in London was

15.6 per thousand, but in Dublin it was 22.3 per thousand.

In 1911 there was a National Census and it recorded that a mind-blowing 835 people lived on one street, Henrietta Street, where this book is set. Nineteen different families lived in number seven – 104 people in total all in one house! In the census it recorded that one family, the Dixons, lost seven of their thirteen children to illness or accidents.

HOW WERE THE TENEMENTS CREATED?

A tenement boy with an injured foot.

In 1801 the Act of Union happened – this meant that the Irish government buildings in Dublin were closed and all the politicians moved to Westminster, in London, where they would now work (representing Ireland from afar) in the British Houses of Parliament.

As well as the politicians, many other Anglo-Irish gentry moved out of Dublin, leaving their grand Dublin homes behind them.

The houses were often bought very cheaply as no one wanted such large houses in the middle of the city any more. Workers were moving to Dublin from the countryside to

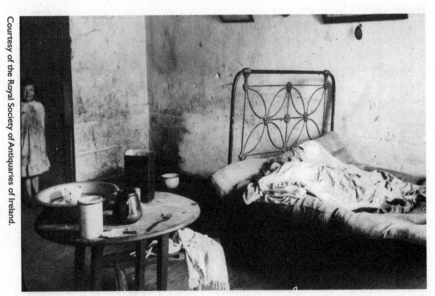

A tenement room at no 38 Francis Street; you can see two children, one in bed, one in the doorway.

find work, especially during the Famine years (1840s) and these grand houses were put to new use – they were broken up into tenement flats by greedy landlords and crammed full of families who needed a roof over their heads.

Many of these old houses had leaky roofs, broken windows, cracked or rotting floorboards and dangerous open fireplaces to cook over and heat the rooms. Their landlords did not look after their properties and people didn't want to complain in case their rent was raised.

THE 14 HENRIETTA STREET MUSEUM

This award-winning museum tells the story of three hundred years in the life of the house, which started off as a grand Georgian house before being divided into tenements. It tells the story of the people who lived in the building and is a brilliant place to visit if you are interested in history.

www.14henriettastreet.ie

THE CHURCH STREET COLLAPSE

The tenement collapse in this book was inspired by the terrible Church Street collapse of 1913. Seven people, including babies and children, lost their lives when two tenement

Number 46 Beresford Street, showing some of the remains of the collapsed houses on Church Street.

buildings fell down.

Edward Joyce had been in one of the buildings, but luckily managed to escape. He said: 'I heard a cracking noise in the wall separating the two houses. I turned round and noticed a stir in the mantelpiece as if it were going to tumble out. … there was a swaying of the wall, and … I darted into the street.'

There was a Housing Inquiry held to find out what happened. It discovered that members of Dublin Corporation – the very people who were supposed to be inspecting the tenements and keeping them safe – were tenement owners.

In the 1930s the tenements were cleared and many families were moved to new houses just outside Dublin city, in places like Crumlin and Ballyfermot. However, some people stayed in their Georgian tenement houses until the 1970s.

HOUSING ISSUES NOW

Many families still don't have a home to live in. According to Focus Ireland there are around 8,000 homeless people in Ireland in 2021, and over 2,000 of these are children. These children live in emergency homeless accommodation with their families. Organisations like Focus Ireland are working to make sure every person in Ireland has a place to call home.

You can find out more here: www.focusireland.ie

THE HISTORY OF CIRCUS IN IRELAND

T he Wilde's Circus in this book is a fictional English travelling circus, but there is a great tradition of circus in Ireland. The second circus in the world was in Dublin. It was set up by Philip Astley in 1773 after he had problems getting a licence to perform in London.

Some of the performances took place in a theatre in Capel Street. They included 'Learned [trained] Dogs', 'Lofty Tumblers' and most exciting of all, Mrs Astley's 'Swarms of Bees'

Patty Astley, Philip's wife, was a famous bee-charming circus artist. She rode around the ring with bees on her neck and arms and is the inspiration for Madam Ada in this book. There was an open-air riding school on Inns Quay, near where the Four Courts now stands, where Mr Astley put on shows featuring his horses and gave riding lessons. He also put on shows at Smock Alley Theatre and in 1798 Mr and Mrs Astley opened their Royal Amphitheatre on

Peter Street, near Christchurch. The Astleys are sometimes called the 'Father and Mother of Circus'.

In 2018 the National Gallery of Ireland ran a special exhibition marking and celebrating 250 years of circus called 'Art of the Show'.

Famous Irish circuses include Fossett's Circus and Duffy's Circus.

FURTHER READING

I found the following books very useful for my research. If you'd like to find out more about Dublin around 1911 they are a great place to start.

Dublin Tenement Life: an Oral History by Kevin C. Kearns is a wide-reaching book about the Dublin slums over the years, full of interviews and first-hand accounts from people who lived there. Age 13+

Darkest Dublin by Christiaan Corlett brings the story of the Church Street disaster alive in vivid detail, using reports and John Cooke's original photographs from the Dublin Housing Inquiry in 1913. It is out of print, but you might find a copy in your local library. Age 13+

Dublin 1911, edited by Catriona Crowe, is a brilliant book that brings the year alive using the National Archives' 1911 census. It's full of photographs, newspaper cuttings and bits and pieces from the time. Age 13+ but many chapters could be shared with readers of age 9+.

Dublin 1913 by Gary Granville is also excellent. Age 11+.

ACKNOWLEDGEMENTS

Many kind people helped me with the research for this book, but any mistakes are mine and mine alone!

I'd like to thank Mary Muldowney, Dublin City Council Historian in Residence for reading my manuscript and being so generous with her time and expertise.

Juno Muldowney also read the manuscript and gave me some terrific and most useful feedback. She also sent me some wonderful Henrietta Street-inspired artwork.

Olly Nolan from Olly's Farm checked the bee facts for me and I'm very grateful for his input. Olly has 180 hives all over Dublin and Wicklow and produces delicious honey. www.ollysfarm.ie

Thomas G. Newman's *Bees and Honey*, published in 1882, gave me the inspiration for the bee facts.

Professor Vanessa Toulmin first told me about Patty Astley and her bee-charming circus act, for which I am forever grateful. Her booklet *What is Circus Today?* is an invaluable and fascinating resource for anyone interested in the history of the circus.

https://www.sheffield.ac.uk/polopoly_fs/1.811639!/file/
WhatisCircusToday.pdf

You can read the National Gallery *Circus 250 Art of the Show* booklet here:

https://www.nationalgallery.ie/sites/default/files/2018-06/
Circus250-Art-of-the-Show-Exhibition-Brochure-final.
pdf

Thanks as always to my wonderful editor, Helen Carr, and all the team at O'Brien Press for their support, patience and enthusiasm, and to Rachel Corcoran for her terrific cover and illustrations.

My dear friend, Tanya Delargy helped with Madam Ada's Italian. *Grazie*!

To my bookish friends: Judi Curtin, for her wisdom and kindness, Martina Devlin and Marita Conlon-McKenna, fellow writers and Irish history fans, and Liz Morris who has listened to a lot of tenement stories over the past two years. Hats off to you all!

And finally, thanks to all the young writers in my writing clubs for working so hard and being so inspirational and to Eve McDonnell, my fellow teacher. To Reese, Julianne,

Isla, Florence, Clodagh, Sara, Rekha, Aimee, Liliana, Eva, Shannon, Sophie, Ash, Sadhbh, Mia, Myles, Faye, Amelia, Lola Mae, Ronith, Maria, Grace, Nishna, Leah, Sabine, Sanika, Niamh, Saoirse, Dylan, Jack, Luke, Hugh, Michael, Isabella, Ysandra, Nessa, Molly, Emilia and Ellie. Keep writing, keep dreaming and keep watching the world with 'glittering eyes'.

OTHER BOOKS
BY SARAH WEBB

FROM THE O'BRIEN PRESS

Blazing a Trail
Irish Women Who Changed the World
Written by Sarah Webb, Illustrated by Lauren O'Neill

Salute the remarkable Irish women who changed
history in this beautifully illustrated book. From Irish
women who made changes in Ireland to those who made
changes abroad. From adventurers to inventors; explorers to
warriors; from designers to writers; rebel leaders to
presidents, this book is a true celebration of Irish women.

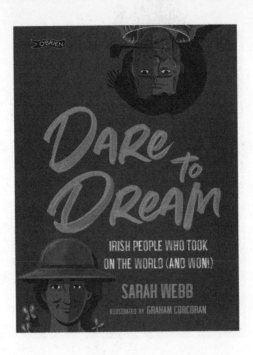

Dare to Dream
Irish People Who Took on the World
(and Won!)

Written by Sarah Webb, Illustrated by Graham Corcoran

Adventurers, explorers, inventors, dreamers: for a small
country Irish people have had a huge impact internationally,
from helping street children in India, to saving Jewish
children during World War II and exploring new worlds.
From Michael Collins to Rosie Hackett, Lady Gregory
to Tom Crean.